THE LITTLE RED BOOK OF
FLY FISHING

"With *The Little Red Book of Fly Fishing*, Deeter and Meyers have joined the hallowed ranks of Penick and Shrake (*Harvey Penick's Little Red Book*) and Strunk and White (*The Elements of Style*) as co-creators of *the* must-have brief bible of a particular métier."

—Monte Burke, author of *Sowbelly: The Obsessive Quest for the World Record Largemouth Bass.*

"Cogent, concise, and continuously entertaining, *The Little Red Book of Fly Fishing* will help you improve your game and, along the way, eek out more enjoyment from the sport. Whatever your skill level when you pick up this slim but wise book, you'll be a better angler after reading it—and referring back to it—as I have."

—Joe Healy, Associate Publisher, *Fly Rod & Reel*

THE LITTLE RED BOOK OF
FLY FISHING
250 TIPS TO MAKE YOU A BETTER TROUT FISHERMAN

**Kirk Deeter
and
Charlie Meyers**

Skyhorse Publishing

Skyhorse Publishing books may be purchased in bulk at special discounts for sales promotion, corporate gifts, fund-raising, or educational purposes. Special editions can also be created to specifications. For details, contact the Special Sales Department, Skyhorse Publishing, 307 West 36th Street, 11th Floor New York, NY 10018 or info@skyhorsepublishing.com.

Skyhorse® and Skyhorse Publishing® are registered trademark of Skyhorse Publishing, Inc.®, a Delaware corporation.
www.skyhorsepublishing.com

14

Library of Congress Cataloging-in-Publication Data
Meyers, Charlie.
  The little red book of fly fishing : 250 tips to make you a better fisherman / Charlie Meyers and Kirk Deeter.
     p. cm.
  Includes bibliographical references and index.
  ISBN 978-1-60239-981-5 (alk. paper)
  1. Fly fishing. I. Title.
  SH456.M487 2010
  799.12'4--dc22
                                      2009046448
Printed in China

THIS BOOK IS
DEDICATED TO
SARAH DEETER AND
DIANNA MEYERS, WHO SHARE
OUR LOVE FOR WILD RIVERS
AND MAKE OUR TIME THERE
MORE COMPLETE.

Contents

Contents

Contents

Contents

Fish sense, applied in the field, is what the old Zen masters would call enlightenment: simply the ability to see what's right there in front of you without having to sift through a lot of thoughts and theories and, yes, expensive fishing tackle.

— John Gierach

Acknowledgments

We'd like to acknowledge Jay Cassell for taking this project under his expert editing wing; Tim Romano for his continued partnership and outstanding photographic contributions; our colleagues at *Field & Stream* and *The Denver Post*; and, of course, our families and fly-fishing friends for their steadfast support.

THE LITTLE RED BOOK OF
FLY FISHING

Introduction

How this book came to be . . .
  I've only known Charlie Meyers since 2002. In that short time, he's become one of my best friends and my outdoor writing mentor.

Our first contact was a cold call. I'd moved to Colorado from Philadelphia, had cowritten a book on fly fishing guides (called *Castwork*), and then found myself in the unenviable position of being an author-turned–self-publicist. With great trepidation, I picked up the phone and dialed Charlie at his *Denver Post* office, intending to beg for some attention to my book. I knew Charlie Meyers was an outdoors writing icon, but it would be a few more years before I'd learn that he'd been writing fishing and hunting stories for the *Post* (in arguably the most "outdoorsy" metro market in America) since 1966, the year I was born.

To my surprise, Charlie picked up the phone, and said, "Yes, I have your book right here. I think it's interesting. We should go fishing together and talk about it."

And we did. Not long after that, he wrote a nice review of my book in the *Post*. We stayed in touch. We fished some more. I wrote another book. And for some reason only Charlie might explain, he saw fit to take me under his wing and teach me about outdoor writing, and fly-fishing writing in particular. We had regular lunch dates and fished together when we could. Sometimes I was the prop figure in stories he'd write for the *Post*. All along the way, at every stop, he gave advice. And I listened.

All of this eventually led me to an editor-at-large position with *Field & Stream* magazine, the world's leading outdoors publication. In time, Charlie and I found ourselves being invited to cover the same events and stories; he for the *Post*, me for *Field & Stream*.

There was one special moment when we were wheeling home toward Denver after fishing the South Fork of the Snake River in Idaho. It was the middle of an August night. I was driving Charlie's Jeep on I-80 outside of Laramie, Wyoming, bleary-eyed and exhausted. Charlie was sleeping in the passenger seat. I reached into the glove compartment to find a cassette, plugged it into the tape deck, and cranked the volume to keep myself awake. Buffalo Springfield . . . "Bluebird." Rolling through the dry wash, I sang the refrain . . . "Do you think, she loves you . . ." And then, Charlie chimed in from his apparent slumber, in perfect harmony . . . "Do you think, at all?"

We decided to write a book together—a book that, like the music, might resonate among different generations. The book would be about fly fishing, the passion that fuels both our souls. (We both also write about bird hunting, big game hunting, and other types of fishing, but when all is said and done, the essential passion for both of us is fly fishing.)

But what did we have to offer? Yes, we both had stories we could tell about our respective adventures, fishing across the country or around the world. The more we talked about the book, though, the more we realized that what mattered most were the tips and tricks we'd learned over the years, things that actually might help people catch fish on the fly. With Charlie's insights from having traveled the world and rubbed shoulders with icons of the sport like Lefty Kreh and Lee Wulff, and with the many ideas I'd gotten from my wild *Field & Stream* adventures, fishing with top guides from Alaska to Tierra del Fuego, we figured we could put together a book like nothing else on the market.

An important aspect of being a fly-fishing writer is that you must live it and do it to be successful. To be a great beat writer covering the National Football League, you really needn't have worn the pads or seen game action. To be a successful political reporter, you need not have actually run for political office. But to be a successful outdoors writer, it's imperative that you not only talk the talk, but also walk the walk.

Both Charlie and I believe that too many self-professed experts have made too much money complicating this sport. In reality, fly fishing is a lot simpler than many people think. You don't have to know the Latin names of every insect, nor do you need to make 70-foot casts, in order to enjoy yourself. The true path to enjoying fly fishing lies in every angler's spirit.

Years ago, I fancied myself a golfer, and I subscribed to the golf magazines, took lessons, and did everything I could to knock a few strokes off my game. Ultimately, I found Harvey Penick's *Little Red Book* on golf to be a great resource. Its plainspoken advice, minus the swing physics and complicated theories, took strokes off my handicap. It's a sensible, no-nonsense book.

Charlie and I have tried to follow that same simple template for fly fishing. In effect, all we have done is opened our notebooks and taken out the best tidbits of advice we could find.

This book is by no means meant to be the ultimate treatise on the rights and wrongs of fly fishing (there are too many of those already . . . and frankly, the more you fish, the more you realize there are no true rights and wrongs). It isn't meant to be a straight-up textbook, either. All it is, is a collection of straight advice, drawn from both of our notebooks (which really exist), intended to help you catch fish on the fly.

To be clear, we've ended every entry with a "K.D." or "C.M." so you will know the source. In some cases, my tips may seem very similar to Charlie's. We elected to run both anyway, as there are usually mild differences, or extra tips, in these situations. But, in the end, we speak with the same voice and have the same convictions, ones that we believe transcend generations. In the end, we also share a single purpose: to help you catch more trout. And maybe, just maybe, you'll feel compelled to start your own notebook, with tips, tactics, and stories that future generations will be able to enjoy.

—Kirk Deeter, *September 2009*

A few weeks after making final edits to our manuscript for The Little Red Book of Fly Fishing, *my friend and partner, Charlie Meyers, died from non-smoker's lung cancer.*

He fought this disease with grace and resolve, and was committed to seeing this project to fruition. Anyone who knew Charlie will agree that his words in this book will ultimately represent only a tiny fraction of his great legacy. The fact that I got to work with and learn from Charlie Meyers was one of my life's greatest blessings. My wish is that all of us honor Charlie's memory by sharing his wisdom and passion for the outdoors with many future generations.

—Kirk Deeter, *January 2010*

PART ONE

The Cast: 45 Tips to Help You Cast Straighter, Longer, and More Accurately

There is no such thing as the perfect cast. There are only casts that catch fish and casts that do not.

In trout fishing, how your cast takes shape doesn't really matter as much as presentation, reading water, and fly selection. The opposite is true in saltwater fly fishing, where the cast is critical. I've often thought that saltwater fly fishing and trout fly fishing are two entirely different sports played with the same basic equipment.

You may have heard the golf adage, "You drive for show and putt for dough." The same is basically true with fly fishing for trout. Sexy loops might impress onlookers, but the fish do not care how well you cast the fly; at least, not nearly as much as they care about how those flies are presented.

When I guide, I see so many people—from amateurs to self-professed experts—seize up and fail, often trading the perfect "could have been" false cast for the imploded "damnit" cast, simply because they're paying too much attention to perfection in the air and not enough to perfection on the water surface.

The key is to relax. The cast is ultimately a game of feel, and your feel will be different from others. Find your own rhythm. Find your own stroke. There are guidelines and tips that can help you down the path of finding the cast that serves you best, but achieving that cast only comes with practice. Definitely study the mechanics of good casting, and work hard to throw consistent, tight loops. Try to eliminate the tailing loops. Being able to throw a long, beautiful fly cast will never hurt you. But that's not a prerequisite for being a good trout angler, no matter what anyone tells you.

In my experience, taking the pressure off yourself is the first step to becoming a good caster. Do that (and absorb these tips that follow), and the cast will come to you, sooner rather than later. —**K.D.**

1. Dare to Be Different

Take a close look at professional golfers the next time there's a tournament on television. Although they shoot similar scores, you'll see surprising variations in swings. Some differences can be laid to body type or perhaps age, the rest to techniques and habits developed over the years.

The same is true with fly casting. Although there exists what might be termed a classic stroke, much like Tiger Woods's golf swing, you can use a variety of techniques to get the fly where it has to go. Certain physical laws pertaining to loading and unloading the fly rod must be adhered to, and timing is critical no matter what your stroke looks like. But if your casting is different from that of your buddy, that's not a problem. It just has to work for you, not anyone else. —**C.M.**

2. It Starts with the Grip

In golf, nine out of ten swing flaws can be traced to your hands and how you hold the club. The same is true of the fly cast. It starts in your grip. You want to be firm, without over-clutching the handle. The line goes where the rod tip

directs it to go, and your grip dictates the direction of the rod tip. Because of this, line your hand up so that it can control how the rod flexes. Hold your thumb on the top of the grip, then snap those casts. If you visualize looking "through" your casting thumbnail, odds are that the line will unfurl right through that window. —**K.D.**

3. **Point Your Shots**

It's axiomatic that the fly line, and thus the fly, follows the rod tip. Taking that one step further, the rod tip follows the thumb, which is the strongest digit and the one most anglers place on top of the grip for power and direction. Lee Wulff used to cast with his index finger on top of the grip because he felt it gave him better control. He was the exception to the rule. No matter. So long as long as you keep your thumb—or index finger—pointed straight for the target, your cast will go where it's supposed to go. —**C.M.**

4. "10 and 2" Is Too Little, Too Late

Many fly-casting instruction books tell you to imagine casting as if your rod moves along an imaginary clock face, with the forward cast stopping at ten o'clock on the imaginary dial and the backcast stopping at the two o'clock position. That's correct, *in theory*. In reality, when casting, most people are oblivious to the positions of that imaginary clock. What feels like two o'clock on the backcast may actually be four o'clock. When I guide, I change time zones and suggest to clients to go to one o'clock on the backcast. For whatever reason, most people achieve the ten o'clock–two o'clock mechanics if they're thinking 10 and 1.

Try it—you'll see what I mean. —**K.D.**

5. Don't Get Cocky

The number-one mistake most novice fly casters make is going back too far on the backcast. The only tipoffs are the noises of line slapping the water or the rod tip scraping the ground behind them. This happens, more often than not, because the caster is allowing his wrist to cock too far back.

As it relates to fly casting, the wrist-versus-arm equation is a difficult balance to describe. Remember this: The arm is the engine; the wrist is the steering wheel. Yes, sometimes it's "all in the wrist," but that pertains to matters of aiming the cast, not powering it. When you let your wrist power your cast, you will inevitably crash.

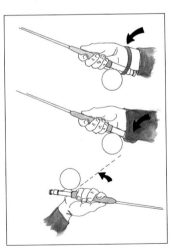

If you have a problem with your wrist over-cocking, there are a few simple fixes that will help you capture the right feel. One is to get a large, thick rubber band, wrap it around your casting wrist, and then insert the rod butt inside that rubber band when you practice casting. If you find that the rubber band is flexing too much, odds are you are breaking your wrist too far.

If you are wearing a long-sleeved shirt, tuck the rod butt inside your cuff. It will have the same effect, and it will tell you when you're cocking your wrist too far on the backcast. Even seasoned anglers will tuck the butt end of their rods inside their shirt cuffs now and again to help them regain their stroke. —**K.D.**

6. Stop! In the Name of Love (and a Good Cast)

When we watch casting, we are absorbed by motion: the back and forth motions of the rod, the fluid flow of the line trailing behind in symmetrical loops. Done correctly, it's a spectacle of motion, one that makes fly fishing so visually appealing.

Always remember that the stop is a key component, one that makes all that casting motion work. A good cast is built by gradually accelerating the rod forward, and stopping it, precisely, then changing direction and gradually accelerating the rod backward, and stopping it again to change course. With each stop, you let out more line. With more line, you exaggerate the time between stops.

If you don't stop the rod crisply on the forward and backward strokes—if you just slush and slop your way forward and back, with no precise rhyme or reason—you cannot load the rod. Your cast will droop, sag, flutter, and die.

The stop is as important a concern as any motion or power in your cast. Stop with authority, forward and back, and you will cast farther, straighter, and more accurately. —**K.D.**

7. **Hitting the Wall**

You've heard the old expression about going after something hammer and tong. To learn how to fully load and unload the rod, instead think hammer and nail.

Loading the rod requires definitive stops and starts. One way to achieve this is to imagine yourself tight between two walls, with nails on both. Using a two-headed hammer, pretend to smack the nails, first on the back cast, and again when the hand comes forward. Each time you hit the nail, the hammer stops cold.

In fly casting, this causes the rod to unload briskly, much in the way a flexed pole propels a vaulter over the bar. The line shoots forward powerfully, with a tight loop. Lacking hard stops and starts, the line loses speed and distance and the loop opens up, making it susceptible to wind. To get full power from your rod, hit the nail on the head. —**C.M.**

8. **Throw a Drink in My Face**

The best description of the gradual, controlled acceleration motion that is the foundation for any good fly cast was offered up by Steve Rajeff, arguably the best caster and all-around angler to ever pick up a fly rod. He said to imagine throwing a glass of water (or beer, if you're so inclined) toward another person. You don't just chuck it. You lift it off the table, accelerate as you aim, and then stop suddenly to let the liquid fly. Imagine doing that when you make your cast and, while you might not fling the line as far as Steve does, you will cast with more distance and accuracy. —**K.D.**

9. Take a Bow

The essence of power casting lies in the precision and speed with which the angler rotates the rod at the apex of the delivery. Call it turnover, tipping the rod over, whatever term you choose. Perform this motion quickly, precisely, and the rod unloads with full power, flinging the line forward with optimum speed.

But what do you do when you lose that timing, when your back cast starts to collapse and things seem to fall apart from fatigue or inattention? To rest your arm and recover the feel, lower your elbow and bring your arm closer to your body.

Instead of trying for power with a tired arm, bend briskly forward at the waist at the point of delivery. Do this, and you'll soon find that your timing and speed will start to

return. Bending, or bowing, with the cast is also an excellent way to add power for distance casting with the arm at full extension. —**C.M.**

10. Watch That Thumb

Many people are frustrated when their line bunches and dies on the forward cast. This is usually caused by going too far with the backcast, which creates an open loop.

The best tip I've ever heard for correcting this came from Dan Stein, a guide on the Bighorn River in Montana. He simply suggests that you keep your casting thumb in your peripheral vision at all times. Lose sight of your thumb, and you're going back too far. Simple as that. —**K.D.**

11. Say Hello to Good Casting

Colorado casting instructor Dan Wright uses this teaching aid to get his students used to starting and stopping the rod at the correct angles: Imagine you're answering an old wall telephone, standing a couple feet away. Say hello when you bring your rod hand smartly back beside your ear, keeping your arm perpendicular, and then whisper good-bye as the phone returns to the cradle. Again, perform this with crisp stops and starts. —**C.M.**

12. William Tell Overture

The rainbow trout, a good one, rises deliberately and persistently in a quick current beneath an overhanging limb just a few feet away. Another tree, close behind, prevents even the wildest thought of a backcast.

The solution? Get a firm grasp on the fly, taking care to avoid the barb, and hold it low to the water. Now, keeping the fly rod tight in the other hand, thrust the rod tip forward with maximum bend while still holding the fly. Next, release the fly quickly while flicking the rod tip forward. The fly will shoot ahead to the full extension of the loose leader, dip neatly beneath the branch, and settle lightly into the feeding lane. The unsuspecting trout, a fish that never could have been approached any other way, eagerly slurps the fly.

Most veteran anglers know this as the bow-and-arrow cast, and it works in more situations than you can imagine. Practice it, and you'll be able to present your fly accurately in many tight situations. —**C.M.**

13. Tighten the Loop

It's a fly-casting axiom: short stroke equals tight loop, long stroke equals lazy loop. One yields power, accuracy, and a precise turn of the leader that also resists the wind. The other? It's okay for short casts and certain situations with lots of weight on the leader or fly. Otherwise, you'll get nothing but trouble from a broad loop.

A beginning caster may be confused when watching a veteran use an extended arm motion when aiming for great distance. The long motion allows for the extreme length the line travels back and forth. The key is the power stroke, that magic moment when the rod tips over at a point near the angler's ear.

It's the quick, short turn during that power application that yields strength and distance. —**C.M.**

14. Anticipation . . . It's Crazy

This happens to all of us. While preparing to make a long delivery, we build momentum through a series of smooth, lengthening false casts. Then, when it's time to let the cast go, everything seems to come apart.

The problem? That old bugaboo called *anticipation*. In our eagerness to get the most out of the delivery, we try to produce too much. That smooth motion collapses into an ill-timed explosion of muscle that completely destroys the form of the cast.

Casting guru Lefty Kreh describes it as "jumping out of your shorts." The solution? Keep your delivery as smooth and even as with your false casts. Don't punch it when you don't need to. Don't try to do too much. —**C.M.**

15. Groove Your Swing

A cast isn't about muscle, it's about tempo and timing. To groove that tempo, try piling 30 to 40 feet of line out the tip of your rod, directly in front of you, at your feet. Next, cast the rod back and forth until you pick up all the line, first with short strokes, then with longer, paused strokes. The line won't stay airborne unless your timing is right. If you are still tangling, that's usually a tailing loop, caused by punching the rod too hard on the forward cast. When you learn how to lift

that pile of line a few feet at a time, you're actually grooving your swing. With enough practice, it becomes second nature. —**K.D.**

16. See the "U"

Watching how your line behaves during the cast will tell you if you're making mistakes. It's tricky to self-diagnose the exact nature of a problem, however, and even harder to make the fix.

Before you get bogged down in complicated physics lessons, try watching your casts from a fresh perspective. Dan Wright taught me this exercise:

To help develop the proper feel for a cast, first tilt your rod sideways and cast from waist or chest level on a flat plane above the ground. Use a measuring tape stretched straight along the ground as your benchmark. Start with small flicks of line, maybe 15 feet long. As you look at the line shooting back and forth, you'll be able to see and feel both good U-shaped loops and tailing loops. Make both forward and backward casts from a dead stop. Eventually, link those casts together. Build line length gradually. As the good loops become uniform and systematic, you'll be able to lift that cast 90 degrees over your head, still watching, and feeling, how the line shapes. If you tail, start

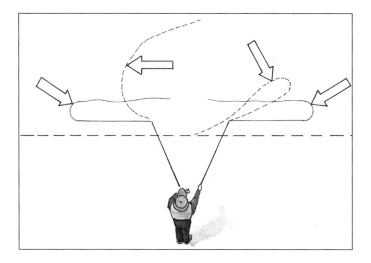

over. The key is keeping the tempo even. Good loops grow in distance with practice. —**K.D.**

17. Flick the Tomato

As we said, the best casting motion involves a gradual, controlled acceleration to an abrupt stop. That's easier said than done, so imagine it this way: If you have a tomato stuck on the end of a stick, and you want to fling that tomato into a bucket 20 feet away, how would you do it? If you whip the stick, you'll end up covered in ketchup. If you gradually fling the tomato off the stick, you might get it there. Same deal and same feel with the fly cast. —**K.D.**

18. Tossing the Grape

Another way to consider this same process is to think of the cast as similar to tossing a grape that's stuck on the tines of a fork. To achieve optimum projection, you stop the fork abruptly at a forward angle, about ten o'clock. —**C.M.**

19. Tuck It In

Your aim is wild, and you can't stroke a consistent path with the line. This happens to a lot of us. Don't worry; this can be fixed. The problem is most likely that your casting arm is flailing. Fly casting isn't like pitching a baseball. To practice your cast, embrace a compact, short stroke by tucking a copy of the Sunday paper in your armpit, under your casting arm. If you drop the paper, your arm is wobbling too wide. —**K.D.**

20. **Too Much, Too Soon**

Perhaps the most common casting error, apart from breaking the wrist on the backcast, comes at the very beginning. Many anglers begin applying full power on the pickup, starting with the rod parallel to the water, while there is still slack line on the water surface. This immediately creates an extremely large loop while failing to properly load the rod. The angler spends the remainder of the cast sequence fighting to tighten the loop, eliminate wind resistance, and build line speed. Most often, he never recovers.

An effective cast begins by stripping in *excess* line, then smoothly lifting the rod tip to ten o'clock. This places the rod in position to load while setting the stage for a short, quick power stroke. Remember: The shorter the power stroke, the tighter the loop and the more powerful the cast. —**C.M.**

21. **The Water-Load**

I was enjoying an autumn afternoon of driftboat hopper fishing on the Yellowstone River with guide Rusty Vorous. My problem was that my cast was consistently coming up about six feet short of trout wedged along the banks. As a team, we had two options: Rusty could row us closer, and risk spooking the fish, or I could muster up the missing distance.

Rusty suggested a simple solution for my problem. The key was having me start my backcast with a taut line and the rod tip pointed low, toward the river surface. In doing so, he taught me to let water resistance and frictional force load the rod.

When you start to cast with your rod tip pointed straight in the air, there's less resistance, no instant energy source to tap into, and no initial rod flex, which ultimately shortens the cast or requires more unnecessary false casting.

"Start it low, and watch it go," Rusty said. "When you load the rod from the water surface, you give your cast a head start." This is a particularly useful tip, not only when you're covering trout water, but also in certain saltwater situations, such as banging repeat long casts into the mangroves, looking for snook. It also helps you form an instant tight loop that cuts through windy conditions. —**K.D.**

22. **Let the Current Do the Dirty Work**

A moving river current can be your best friend when it comes to avoiding tangles, setting up casts, loading the rod, and taking your best shot. Understand that in good conditions, a 20- or 30-foot cast is often long enough to produce results. As such, when I guide, I have a system for coaching people who have never held a fly rod in their lives. If you let the water do the dirty work—meaning let the current load the rod—even a beginner can make accurate casts, avoid tangles, and catch fish.

Stand perpendicular to the current, and toss your line in front of you so that it feeds out the end of the rod to a desired length as the water moves your fly downstream. When your line is extended, and your fly is in the current downstream, skittering on the surface (this sometimes catches fish, by the way, so pay attention), simply lift the rod tip to the sky and lock it in that two o'clock position. Stop! Wait.

Now fix your eyes upstream on the target area you want to cast toward. Bring the rod forward, snap it to a stop, and aim through your thumb. The fly line will unfurl and your fly will (usually) land right in the zone.

The key is the pause. Let the line stretch. Let the fly skitter. Lift the tip. Set it up, and let it fly. Not pausing and not letting the current load the rod is a tangle waiting to happen.

Call it a super-slow-motion roll cast, a beginner's trick, whatever. No matter how good you get, you'll find yourself false casting less and letting the currents work for you more often. —**K.D.**

23. Roll 'Em Easy

I find that I roll cast on a river at least three times for every overhead cast I make. When you get the roll cast down and you learn to use the water to load your rod, you'll find yourself spending less time and energy thinking about casting. In turn, you'll be more focused on reading the water and finding fish.

The roll cast is important for two other reasons. First, it's a stealthier approach and is less likely to spook fish than false casting overhead. Second, it's your go-to option when there are bushes or other obstacles behind you, where they'll likely foul up a backcast.

What's the key to a good roll cast? Same as with any other cast—gradually accelerate the rod, building speed and resistance, then stop, change direction, and unfurl the cast forward.

A common mistake people make is to start that roll cast with too much loose line on the water and the rod tip pointed straight at the sky. Instead, retrieve with the rod tip from a low position, with noticeable tension on the line as it slices through the current. When the moment is right (and you'll develop a feel to know when), lift the rod tip skyward and snap the rod forward, unfurling an on-target cast. —**K.D.**

24. Saving a Stroke

When roll-casting or making a roll pickup, save an extra motion—and thus time and a potential foul-up—with this tactic. With a lot of line still on the water, lower the rod tip near the surface and rotate it backward. Surface tension on the line will cause those loose coils accumulated around your feet to slide out through the guides, adding several feet to the line already in play and eliminating at least one false cast. As a bonus, this motion places the rod and line in the perfect loading position to deliver the cast. Done properly, this technique can eliminate false casts entirely. —**C.M.**

25. The Woody Hayes Rule of Casting

Legendary Ohio State football coach Woody Hayes once explained why he closely embraced the "three yards and a cloud of dust" offensive philosophy this way: "When you put the ball in the air, three things can happen, and two of them are bad." Whether or not the coach actually said those words (the quote has also been attributed to Duffy Daugherty and others), it got me thinking about the obvious correlation with fly casting.

While beautiful long loops might be pleasing to watch, they usually don't do a lot for you on the trout stream. False casts spook fish. And all casts have the potential of developing line-weakening wind knots, which occur when an angler cannot control his line. Why not let the current do the work instead? Let the water stretch the line behind you. Lift your rod tip high, pause, then unfurl a pinpoint cast by directing the rod tip where you want your fly to land. The angler who learns how to roll cast, improvises with short mends, adjusts the fly line with the help of the current, and learns to let the water help him set up the next cast is going to be much better off than the one who tries to throw a Hail Mary on every play. While you might not beat that school up north every time you play, you'll commit fewer turnovers, and win your fair share of games. —**K.D.**

26. Forty Feet in Four Seconds

Different folks have tried to invent casting competitions over the years to rate fly fishers. Let's get this straight: Casting competitions rate casters, not anglers. I don't care what anyone says, being able to cast a fly line 115 feet is entertaining, but it is not practically important, especially not in trout fishing. And while throwing flies into a floating hula hoop may be good target practice, it's a far cry from the real deal.

My friend Travis Holeman, who fished the professional redfish tour (but is an all-around angler and a damn good trout fisherman), summed up the difference between a "real-life" good caster and a "for-show" good caster this way: "Give me 40 feet, on target, in four seconds, and you'll catch more fish—I don't care if you're talking redfish, trout, or salmon—than anyone." In other words, factor in timing.

A real test for your angling skills would be to set out a course of targets that are all 40 feet away from you, numbered 1 through 10. Someone calls a number at random, and you have four seconds and one cast to put a fly you're holding in your hand within two feet of that target. Not fast enough, no good. Not close enough, no good.

Work on that little exercise long enough, and when Mr. Brown Trout pokes his head up in the river, you'll be comfortable with what you have to do. Your cast doesn't have to be long—it has to be on target, and on time. *That's* what makes a good caster, and a successful angler. —**K.D.**

27. Come Closer, Darling

Close counts in fly fishing as well as dancing. Even though you may have the ability to deliver a dry fly with reasonable accuracy at distances of 50 feet or more, your chances of actually catching a fish increase dramatically with every inch you can trim off that.

Granted, there are situations where a long cast is essential. But, while hero shots may earn applause from onlookers, they catch trout mostly in magazine stories.

Consider the reasons for shortening the cast: pinpoint accuracy to achieve just the right presentation; less line disturbance on the water; far greater ability to mend and control the drift; faster hook set; and less line to manage after hook up, particularly if the fish is a good one. The list extends to dozens of factors, all of which add up to less casting and more catching.

Of these, drift manipulation is the most important. A shorter line translates to fewer intervening currents between your rod tip and fly, thus a much easier task in maintaining the drag-free drift essential to most presentations.

To make this work, choose an approach that puts you in the best and closest position to work a rising fish or a promising feeding lane. You'll be surprised how close you can approach in moving water. If the water is particularly swift and broken, cut that distance by half.

For example, we can recall many times during a prominent hatch when trout splashed for insects right beneath our rod tips. At first, this might seem frustrating. But there's a powerful message here. The grass isn't necessarily greener, nor the trout larger, on the other side of the river. Why cast to faraway fish when you have feeding fish within easier range? The manifesto for shorter casts goes on and on. Oh, yes. Did we mention fewer snagged limbs, wind knots, and other assorted tangles with a shorter cast? —**C.M.**

28. When Not to Cast (or Even Twitch)

One recent development in fly fishing on still water is the use of strike indicators for presenting nymphs. The concept is to suspend the fly just above bottom vegetation, where fish typically cruise to pick off insects and other organisms. The method succeeds because the fly spends maximum time in the zone where trout are searching. Trout looks for food; trout sees fly; trout eats fly; angler catches fish.

This tactic works best if you don't move the fly at all. Cast to the desired location, let the fly sink, and let it sit. The indicator, acting as a bobber, will hold it in place. In this case, patience is more than its own reward. —**C.M.**

29. Control Trumps Distance

If long casts are needed in certain situations, they will count for little unless they are done accurately and with the precise loop control that's needed to properly present the fly.

"If you don't keep your loop under control, all you're doing is casting your mistakes farther," quips cast master Lefty Kreh. "Some guys are so hung up on distance, they end up casting a bird's nest a robin wouldn't rent."

Kreh's message: Master the form before you try for distance. —**C.M.**

30. Pinkie Perfection

Fly fishers aren't effeminate by nature, but you'll occasionally find someone extending a little finger while casting as if taking a sip at high tea. Not to worry. There's a sound motive behind such a peculiar act. Removing the pinkie from the rod forces the angler to become more thumb-directed, the proper position for keeping the stroke on track when the rod tip starts to wander. To emphasize this effect, also take your ring finger off the grip. Once you've recovered the feel, return to a normal grip. You'll discover that both your power and your accuracy have improved. —**C.M.**

31. Cast around Problems

Some days, satisfaction can be measured as much in the absence of frustration as in the presence of fish. Snagged branches, wind knots, lost flies—most of these problems can be avoided with simple actions.

When getting ready to cast, for example, take a quick look around for potential obstructions before you do. Cross to the other side of the stream to free your casting arm from branches or adverse wind direction. Try roll casting whenever possible.

School yourself in avoiding common hazards. You'll spend more time actually fishing while remaining upbeat and happy, a better posture for success.—**C.M.**

32. Make Friends with the Wind

The windiest place I've ever fished was the redfish flats of Aransas Bay, Texas. It was there, as I was struggling with a flapping fly line, that guide Chuck Naiser called a halt to the action, gently placed his hand on my shoulder, and said, "Son, you're gonna have to make friends with that wind, or else come back here in July when it calms down . . . but all the locals are busy then, chasing down the chickens that blew out of the barnyard." The point was well taken, and using the wind to your casting advantage is especially important for the trout angler who has learned the hard way that breezes whipping through the canyon can mess with the best intentions.

For a right-handed fly caster, the perfect wind is a gentle one coming over the left shoulder, because it keeps your line and flies pushed away from your head at a safe distance. When the wind howls from the right side, tip the top of your rod at a raised angle over your left shoulder, still powering the stroke from your right side. When the wind is directly behind you, shorten and power that backcast high, allowing the fly line to kite up with the wind's force.

If you go too far back, or break your wrist, and let that rod tip dip blow the kite plane, the wind will pile-drive the fly line into the water behind you. But do it correctly, and you'll reap the same rewards as the golfer who finds added driving distance with a tailwind. And the most intimidating wind of all—the

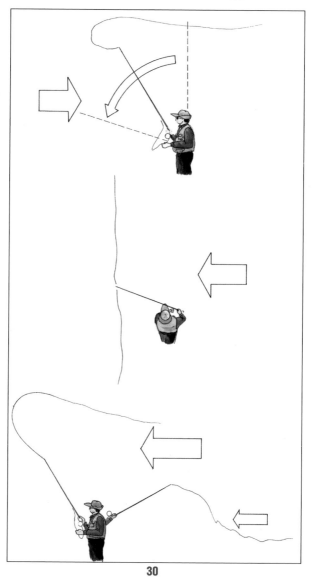

one that blows right in your face—might actually be your ally. After all, your backcast is where you load the power in the rod, and a stiff breeze will help straighten the line behind you. To transfer that energy through the teeth of the wind, make a slight adjustment to finish your forward stroke lower.

In other words, if you normally stop the rod at 10 and 2 on the imaginary clock face, shift to 9 and 1, stopping higher on the backcast, and driving lower on the front. Remember, punching the rod won't get you anywhere but tangled. This isn't a power game; it's about timing. When you can form a tight casting loop, and make small adjustments to counter the effects of wind on the river, you'll never be blown away. —**K.D.**

33. Wind Knots and the Big Bang Theory

Let's get one thing straight: Wind knots aren't caused by the elements; they're caused by what you do. It's okay, they happen to everyone. But I will say this: Early diagnosis is the key to fixing the problem and getting back to business. And I have never, in all my life, seen a tangled mess get fixed by whirling and twirling the rod tip. It might be human nature to try and undo the problem by twirling the rod in reverse motion, but the sooner you learn to stop and address the problem, the better off you are. When I see the intricate mazes of highly complex, patterned knots that result from a micro-second lapse of concentration, it reinforces my belief that this whole delicately balanced universe may have indeed resulted from a massive explosion. —**K.D.**

34. Fast Rods Cover Casting Flaws

Technology is a wonderful thing. And as it has been applied to sports, technology has done wonders to put us all in the game. Look, for example, at tennis racquets and golf clubs. Composite materials, oversize heads (larger sweet spots) . . . get the right gear, and you simply can't lose! Right? Not! It isn't the gear, it's the player, and that's just as true with fly fishing as with other sports. These fast-action rods are great fun, and they do help you add distance to your casts. How? By compensating for errors in your form. When I practice casting, I practice with a slow- or medium-action rod. Then, if I want to kick it up a notch, I use that fast-action rod to my advantage. There is a real benefit to using the latest technologies. They work! But ask yourself what's the real advantage for you: Are you like Tiger Woods, swinging the best clubs because they enhance your beautiful game, or are you using a crutch? Be honest. —**K.D.**

35. The Double Haul

One way to get more distance out of your cast is to use a double haul. This involves using your "off" hand to hold the line and pulling that line, then giving it back, as you make forward casts and backcasts. What this does is increase the resistance and flex in the rod, making the line virtually heavier at the critical moment, and ultimately increasing line speed when you shoot the cast.

It is the hardest technique to teach to any fly caster, because no matter how you describe it, the double haul is ultimately a matter of timing and feel.

The most common mistake is that casters know and feel when to pull down on the line, but they don't give the line back to shoot through the guides. They pull, and then they find themselves with their arms far apart, with slack line that inevitably spoils the cast.

Imagine your hands bungee-corded together. As soon as you make that pull on the backcast, let the imaginary bungee bring your hands closer together, and feel the line slip through your fingers.

The best way to get the feel of the double haul is to start with a mini-haul. Pull just a few inches at a time, with short casting strokes, until you sense the timing.

With practice, you'll find that hauling becomes ingrained in your timing. You'll know how to make strong, sharp hauls when you're booming an 8-weight through the wind on the flats . . . and you may also catch yourself, perhaps subconsciously, mini-hauling as you cast the 3-weight at brookies in a small stream.
—**K.D.**

36. Just a Flick of the Wrist

Little things often make the difference between an average cast and an eye popper. Certified instructor Dan Wright offers this

hint to add a couple long pulls to your distance: The crux move comes at the completion of the double haul. Just when you've finished your normal haul, rotate your wrist sharply downward, ending with your thumb pointing toward the ground. The payoff, Wright assures us, is an extra acceleration that rockets the line through the guides. **—C.M.**

37. **Remove the Shackles**

We've all watched this guy cast. Like a golfer rotating into his backswing, he rocks backward with his hands close together, as if his wrists were in handcuffs. This stroke works well enough with a golf club, which doesn't have a fly line attached to it, but with a fly rod, the line prescribes a lazy sideways loop behind the angler's back. The forward cast often hits him behind the head.

The cure is as simple: Hold the line hand in a relaxed position near the chest, well away from the rod. Keep the body square to the target, both eyes straight ahead. Once the rocking motion has ended and our angler becomes comfortable with the proper stance, he'll be ready to start learning the double haul, an advanced maneuver that actually does involve lifting the line hand up near the reel. **—C.M.**

38. **Lose the Tailing Loop**

The tailing loop is, to a fly fisher, what the slice is to a golfer: a common problem, caused by a simple mechanical flaw. Both can ruin your game. If you are accustomed to playing that second shot from an adjacent fairway or you often find yourself untying wind knots on the riverbank, you probably know what I'm talking about.

Golf pros will blame most slices on open club faces. As for a tailing loop, when the fly and leader dip below your line on the forward cast (usually causing an untimely tangle), the most common cause is overpowering or punching the rod on the forward stroke. Don't feel bad; it's human nature. We've all been there. Trout are rising, I'm making my false casts, I've got a nice loop going, all I need is 10 more feet, so I give it a little more oomph and—pow!—bunched up again.

In physics terms, this is actually caused when the rod tip travels on a *concave* path from the backcast to the forward cast. The line goes where the rod tip tells it to go, and when the rod tip travels a fairly even, flat, and steady path, the loop is uniform. When you overpower the rod, however, you flex it too much and actually shorten its length mid-stroke. That's what causes the rod to launch the line in a flight path where the tip-end tails. —**K.D.**

39. Fish Like a Snake

In the never-ending struggle to steal time from the current while presenting a dry fly, the serpent cast, often called an "S" cast, can be a most valuable tool. The notion is to put several coils or wiggles in the line when completing the forward cast. During the precious seconds it takes for intervening currents to work the coils out of the line, your fly will have extra drag-free float in the target zone.

The "S" cast isn't nearly as difficult as it might seem. Remember that the line always follows the motion of the rod tip. When delivering the cast, simply wiggle the rod tip, like a brush stroke painting coils into the line. This tactic works particularly well when casting directly upstream, but it serves much the same purpose at any angle, as well as for nymphing. With practice, the stroke will become automatic. —**C.M.**

40. Will Your Casts

As with a golf shot, or shooting an arrow from a bow, or even breaking clay pigeons with a shotgun, it's important to visualize where you want the fly cast to go. Taking even an extra half second or so before you let the cast go will help you will your casts into the right spot. Yes, you want to be quick and react to opportunity, but if you can't clearly pick out your target and make a measured cast in that split second—just as you would shooting clay targets—it will be a game of "close but no cigar." —**K.D.**

41. What Spooks Trout

Like many anglers, I often found myself wondering what the fish were actually doing beneath the surface. Eventually, my curiosity got the better of me. I got some scuba gear, dove into the North Fork of the South Platte River in Colorado, and hung out with the trout to watch and learn what was really going on as a couple of my buddies cast flies at the fish. This "be the fish" experience eventually evolved into a story for *Field & Stream* magazine called "Going Deep in the Name of Trout Research."

The most riveting lesson I took away upon resurfacing was that the fish were not startled by my presence among them; I could often get within arm's reach of a feeding trout, and it wasn't bothered one bit by the big, neon, bubble-blowing mass in the water next to it. But any real motion overhead—a bird's shadow, for example—triggered an immediate nervous instinct to scatter or head for deeper water.

That also held true for false casts over the fish. As I held onto a boulder on the river bottom, I watched the fish skitter

away time and time again after my friends started false casting over the run. With every false cast, the wariness intensified, in effect diminishing the possibility of a hookup with each pass the line made over the water.

Think about that in the context of the shadows you cast and the number of times you false cast. Try to keep your false casts to a minimum, and direct them slightly outside of the line of fire, bringing only the cast that counts into the target zone. —**K.D.**

42. The Hard Splashdown Isn't So Bad

I learned a lesson from Terry Gunn of Lees Ferry Anglers in Arizona one afternoon while we were fishing dry flies in Marble Canyon. It's often better to splash your flies down on the surface than it is to make many false casts and create fluttering shadows from your flies and line over the fish.

Think about it. Boom, pop—all of a sudden the fly is there in the fish's feeding lane. Naturally, you do not want to make a lot of commotion, and it's a huge mistake to rip your flies out of the water in close proximity to feeding trout (mayflies typically don't take off with the force of a water rocket). Ideally, you want to elevate your imaginary bull's-eye target a foot or two above the surface, as if you're casting into a hula hoop suspended inches above the water. You want your line, leader, and fly to reach full extension and fall gracefully into that zone.

If I'm going to err on the high side or the low side of that target, however, I'll inevitably err low. —**K.D.**

43. Make the First Cast Count

It sounds simple, but after a guide has seen a client throw wildly into a pod of surface-feeding trout a few hundred times (to no effect), it's worth repeating that you should make your first

cast count as if it were your only and best shot, because often times it is. It's always better to stop, assess, and make the cast you want. Yes, a combination of speed and accuracy is ideal. But if I'm forced to choose one over the other, I always choose accuracy. Ninety-nine times out of 100, speed does not, in fact, trump accuracy when you are fly fishing for trout. —**K.D.**

44. Time Your Casts

If you make a decent cast, and the trout you were after ignores your fly, wait and watch. You'll find that trout eating dry flies are often in a natural rhythm. They feed . . . pause . . . they feed right . . . pause . . . they feed left . . . pause. Pause more. Then they start over, in roughly the same routine. Synch your casting clock with that routine—use your eyes as much as your arm—and the effectiveness of your casting will improve incrementally. —**K.D.**

45. Give Me a Good Drift Over a Good Cast, Any Day

Any good guide will tell you the same thing: In trout fishing, the most important three seconds are those right before and during the time a fly—dry fly or nymph—enters the zone where a trout is eating. In other words, it doesn't matter how you get it there, but when that offering hits the water, it had better look appetizing or you're out of luck. In trout fishing, that means the drift has to be perfect. I don't care if you make a 70-foot flawless cast with a perfect loop, or if you hand-toss the fly, fling it, zip it, chuck it, or deliver it by FedEx; once the fly hits the water, it has to look natural, period. Give me a good drift over a perfect cast, any day, and you'll catch more fish. Promise. —**K.D.**

PART TWO

Presentation: 60 Tips to Help You Place and Drift Your Flies So That Trout Want to Eat Them

When we talk about presentation, we're talking about the most crucial element of fly fishing. How does that fly look to a trout in the instants before it decides to eat it, or not? Granted, with brains the sizes of marbles, trout aren't terribly deep thinkers. But they are critics to the extent that instinct tells them what looks natural and what does not.

Most of the time, but not always, trout only eat things that look natural to them, especially in the fly-fishing arena.

My best anecdote that puts the whole fly presentation issue into perspective is a saltwater fishing story. I was working the flats with Bill Curtis, a legend among south Florida fly guides,

and we saw a big permit cruise into the shallows. I have no idea how big the fish really was; suffice to say it looked like a metal trash can lid shimmering under the surface.

I made what I thought was a perfect cast, about 60 feet, slightly leading the fish, with the fly landing about five feet past the permit. I made a few strips of the line, to skip my crab fly along the bottom into what I thought would be the zone. The permit finned away, more annoyed than spooked.

"What went wrong?" I asked. "I made a great cast. I didn't line the fish. . . . "

Bill picked up his push pole and grumbled down at me on the deck, "Fish aren't used to their food attacking them."

Good point.

Apply that thinking to all your fly fishing, especially trout fishing. An insect—be it a nymph floating under the surface or a dun drying its wings on the surface—is usually moving at the mercy of the current. An emerging insect is swimming toward the surface. A baitfish that senses a predatory trout in its vicinity will swim nervously *away* from the fish.

So the trick with presentation is to make flies act how they're designed to look: dead drift nymphs with the current, with no drag; make spinners fall from the sky and lie almost lifeless on the surface; swim your streamers.

There are times when the rules can be bent: Twitch a grasshopper near a cutbank, dead-drift a Woolly Bugger through a deep run, fish dry flies wet, fish wet flies dry, and so on. But by and large, if you present your flies in a way that makes them *behave* as naturally as possible, all the while keeping your presence as stealthy and blended into the environment as possible, you've discovered the number-one secret to fly-fishing success.

Whether you can cast 20 feet or 120 feet, and whether you have a spot-on matching fly pattern or an old generic standard, what happens in the first seconds after the fly hits the water matters most. Always. —**K.D.**

46. The Dead Drift

When you are dry fly fishing, a good presentation always starts with a good drift. And a good drift is usually a dead drift, meaning the fly is traveling in exact connection with the current.

I once walked up on a guide friend and his client on a gorgeous Colorado afternoon, a day when insects were swarming and the fish were happy.

"What are they eating?" I asked.

"A good drift," he said, smiling.

And to prove the point, he showed me the size 14 Royal Trude his guy was fishing with. I'd seen a lot of bugs that day, but nothing that looked quite like that.

The secret to a good dead drift is casting upstream and letting your fly float with the current. Drag, when the fly line is caught by the current, causing tension that moves the fly unnaturally, and "micro-drag," when the leader does the same thing, will inevitably turn fish off.

Try to keep as little fly line on the water as possible. When the fly is moving from upstream down at a straight tangent, drag is less of a concern. But when you are casting at an angle to the current, keeping the line off the water is smart; failing that, always keep the fly line upstream from the flies. —**K.D.**

47. High-Stick Nymphing

The value of a good dead drift applies to nymph fishing, especially when you use a method called high-stick nymphing (as opposed to European or short-line nymphing). With high-stick nymphing, you typically fish two flies below a split shot, each element separated by about a foot of tippet material. Fasten a strike indicator to your leader a few feet above the weight.

The idea is that the weight drops to the bottom of the river, the flies trail delicately behind, and when a fish grabs a fly, the indicator will tell you by way of a subtle dip or stall on the surface.

Dead drifting your flies, first letting them settle into the run and, as they pass your position, remembering to keep the line upstream from the indicator, is the trick to making this all work. —**K.D.**

48. The Whole Nine Feet

Have you ever wondered why most fly rods are longer than conventional spinning rods? It's because that added length helps you control, cast, and tend your line effectively. So why do I see so many people "mend" their line with forceful strokes, or try to roll cast from hip level? Because they don't know what they are doing. Point the rod tip high in the air when you mend your line. It doesn't take a mighty whip of the line to mend; in fact, whipping the line is the worst thing you can do to your drift.

Lift it and lay it down. Gently.

It's amazing what can happen when you use a full rod length to do what it's designed to do. When you want to roll cast, think about using the rod tip as leverage. Often, the higher you lift, the further you roll. The one exception to the higher is better mode of thinking happens after you've made a good cast, you've mended your line, and your flies are floating perfectly through the run. At that point, I want to keep the rod flat, or parallel, to the water line. Why? Because when the rod is flat above the water line, all it takes is a gentle flick of the wrist to set the hook.

When you drift your flies with the rod tip pointed at the sky, you have no leverage on the fish and no means of finding the resistance necessary to set the hook unless you yank the rod over your shoulder. Use the length of the rod to your advantage. When you cast and mend, keep the tip high. Lift and place. When you drift and set the hook, keep the tip lower. Use all nine feet, every time, every cast, every mend, and every drift.
—**K.D.**

49. Mending Your Ways

Mending—the art of tossing a bend in your line as a hedge against drag—is an essential element for effective drifts. The trick is knowing when and how much. Anglers make two basic mistakes: mending too aggressively and not often enough.

A powerful, sweeping mend while nymphing has the negative effect of lifting the fly off the bottom, often during the sweet spot of the drift. Try to gauge how to mend the line with minimal movement of the fly. With a shorter line, this often can be achieved simply by lifting the rod tip to place the line in the desired position.

Several short mends that don't disturb the fly are better than one big one. Generally, the best time to mend is just *before* you think you really need it. —**C.M.**

50. Finding Your Mark

Since even the slightest drag can spoil the presentation of a dry fly, it's important to know when this occurs. The best way to know if your fly is moving too fast is to mark another object in the immediate vicinity: a leaf, an air bubble, an insect. If your fly is keeping pace, you're in business; moving too fast, then it's time to make a mend. —**C.M.**

51. The Swing

You're fishing nymphs in a run, and just as you get ready to lift up and make another cast—bang—you get a hit! It happens all the time. What you just did is hook a fish on the swing. As the line straightens out down current, the flies inevitably lift

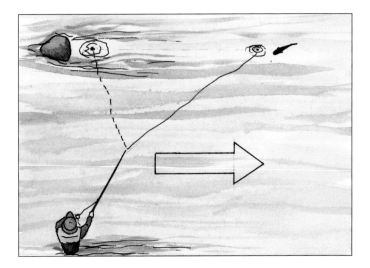

toward the surface, which looks exactly like insects emerging. Trout love eating those bugs.

Many people have lost touch with the art of wet fly fishing and swinging bugs subsurface. In my family, we had a rule that the little kids had to fish the river with wet flies, so they'd work the water going downstream. When you got big enough, you were allowed to turn back into the current and start working dry flies upstream.

I always thought that Grandpa made that rule to keep the kids dry. I'm starting to see an ulterior motive: We caught a lot of fish that way, and learned the value of the swing. —**K.D.**

52. **Doing the Continental**

Extreme short-line nymphing has taken the fly-fishing world by storm, and for this we can thank international angling competitions. Generally known as the European Method, it evolved in Poland or the Czech Republic, depending upon which branch of the Slavic kingdom you happen to be talking to. The technique takes the rationale for shorter casts a giant leap farther, to virtually no cast at all.

The whole idea is to get as close as possible to trout holding in deep currents, which gives you a chance to maintain direct contact with the fly. This means only six feet of leader, starting with 3X and dropping quickly to 5X, and no fly line outside the rod tip. The notion is to position the rod perpendicular, with the tip close to the water, just above the prime holding lie. When a trout bites, you feel it. No missed strikes here. Experts further emphasize this connection by "leading the fly," a ploy by which the line moves every-so-slightly faster than the current—enough to keep tight contact without compromising the natural drift. Tournament veterans say it also pays to give a series of quick hook sets when the fly enters a zone likely to hold fish.

Don't worry too much about spooking fish, as trout seldom flee to the other side of the river. Instead, they typically move away about 10 feet—just about on target for your short-line drift. —**C.M.**

53. Weighty Matters, Part I

On a typical spring day on Wyoming's North Platte River, wind ripped straight downstream hard enough to blow the horns off a goat. What had been a sensational nymph bite for big rainbows suddenly went dead. It took a minute to understand the problem, but the solution was almost instantaneous. This downstream wind greatly accelerated the surface speed of the water, now rushing much faster than where the fly was located, four feet below.

The solution: Move closer and shorten the line, which was now possible because wind rippling the surface makes it difficult for fish to see the angler. Then pinch on two more BB-size split shot, the quickest and best way to slow the drift. The result: The bite immediately returned.

Most nymph fishermen are minimalists when it comes to using lead, choosing the least amount to reach the desired depth. Trouble is, we waste much of the target zone waiting for the fly to sink. Instead, put on twice as much weight as you think you need.

It may not be pleasant to cast, but it catches fish. —**C.M.**

54. Weighty Matters, Part II

When conditions demand a presentation very close to bottom, don't be afraid to shorten the distance between the weight and the fly. Within reason, trout don't seem to care much about this spacing and won't be spooked by the weight. The payoff comes in keeping your fly from floating up out of the zone where fish are holding. Trout are accustomed to a constant barrage of objects in drift. If they got put off by something as small as a split shot, they'd starve to death. —**C.M.**

55. Weighty Matters, Part III

When current, wind, or any combination thereof conspire to keep you from an acceptable nymphing drift, there's one sure cure: Add more weight. Think anvil. As one might imagine, heavy objects are resistant to being moved by water. The more weight you attach to your line, the slower it will move with the flow. —**C.M.**

56. The Difference between a Good Fisherman and a Great One? A BB

I have never met an angler who doesn't like or respect Pat Dorsey. For those of you who do not know Pat, he is, hands down, the hot stick guide on the trout rivers closest to Denver, namely the highly technical Cheesman Canyon section of the South Platte River, the Dream Stream section of the Platte (up in South Park), the Williams Fork of the Colorado (near Kremmling), and pretty much anywhere else he chooses to guide. He literally wrote the book on fly fishing the South Platte.

The fact that Pat is almost uniformly recognized as the best guide in one of the busiest trout fishing regions in America is tall praise. Despite that, he remains humble, hard working, and amazingly open with his bag of tricks. The most important lesson he ever shared came on a crowded day near Deckers—one of those days when conditions were challenging, the fish were stubborn, and the place was packed with so many anglers, we simply didn't have the option of bouncing from one run to the next. We had to make do with the water right in front of us.

Pat tied on a double-nymph rig, with an RS2 and a Black Beauty. Three casts, and nothing. Pat suggested we add a "fuzz" more weight to the rig. A few more casts, and nothing still. I suggested we switch flies, as we knew the run we were working held fish. Maybe they just didn't like our flies. No, insisted Pat, we'll add a little more weight. Several more casts, nothing. He added yet *another* BB and, two casts later, we tied into a hefty brown trout.

That fish had been there all along. We never switched fly patterns. What we did was find the right weight balance that made those flies finally drop perfectly into the trout's feeding zone. It was an offer the fish, ultimately, could not refuse. "Weight," said Pat, "is the most important factor when you are fishing with nymphs. I might cast 100 times with different flies, but if the weight isn't right, it won't work. When the weight is right, the fly will almost always work."

Think about that the next time you're frustrated at the edge of a run you know holds trout. Think about your weight before switching fly patterns. It's probably worth 10 weight adjustments before any single fly change, especially when you are casting at educated and challenging trout. After all, Pat explained, "The difference between a good fisherman and a great one is often no more than a BB." —**K.D.**

57. A Knockout with the Bolo Punch

Think of it as the ultimate risk-reward scenario, only this time the scale tips heavily for the reward. The subject is multiple flies, three for the sake of this discussion. We all know the risk: a wildly spinning gaggle of hooks that becomes more precarious with any addition of weight to the line. Cast improperly, it's like the gaucho's bolo just waiting for a tangle.

Done correctly, it may be the most deadly method for fishing a stream when there's no clearly defined hatch. Start with a bushy, buoyant dry fly on the surface, then drop down to a weighted attractor nymph at the depth you think the best fish will be holding. Using a finer tippet about 10 inches long, attach a small nymph that imitates the primary subsurface insect.

Get this down to the fish and watch your success rate climb. The dry fly serves primarily as an indicator, but don't be surprised if it gets a few grabs along the way.

As for avoiding snarls, let the line drift all the way downstream, and use a river load rather than a backcast. Never allow the line to decelerate on the forward cast. —**C.M.**

58. Seeing the Light

Deep evening shadows had descended on the canyon that cradles the lower Arkansas River before it spills out onto Colorado's southeastern plains. The small Blue-winged Olive dry fly so popular with the river's resident browns had faded from sight in the growing darkness; the angler's offering no longer could be distinguished among the frequent rises to naturals.

Don Puterbaugh, a river guide for 30 years, had the perfect solution. He rigged a larger, white-winged dry fly a couple feet ahead of the tiny mayfly imitation, providing a perfect directional arrow to the target. Trout ignored the big fly while readily eating the small one, which now was easy to locate. The angler enjoyed splendid action almost until dark. —**C.M.**

59. The Thin, Clear Line

Lee Wulff called it far and away the most significant invention in angling history. No, he wasn't talking about the graphite rod or plastic-coated fly line or even leak-proof waders.

The foremost creation, he determined, is monofilament, or, as it pertains to fly fishing, the ultra-fine tippet material that gives us the ability to deceive even the shyest of fish.

A seemingly unending progression of polymers now enables us not only to employ absurdly fine tippets almost invisible in the water, but also to imitate almost microscopic flies. The principal benefit comes in the ability to fish successfully in those difficult places and conditions that hold the most desirable trout.

Flash forward to a western tailwater in mid-January. As a hedge against extreme cold, an angler has pre-rigged with 5X and a size 22 midge larvae to imitate the insects prevalent at this time and place. His companion, more savvy at this location, has tied a No. 26 midge to 6X.

An hour later, the finer offering has produced a half-dozen good trout; the angler with the bigger flies and line has caught nothing. Risking frostbitten fingers, the frustrated angler adds a length of 6X and a smaller fly. He catches a nice trout on the next cast.

While a slender, flexible tippet helps to avoid spooking fish—especially when attached to a tiny fly—the greater benefit lies in allowing flies to move naturally in the current. This is particularly true in clear, slow-moving water. With a bit of practice playing fish, the notion of tying a tiny fly to a 6X tippet no longer should bring trepidation, just more bites. **—C.M.**

60. Live with It

You see a trout rising in a riffle with consistent, steady gulps. You wade into position for a cast, make the perfect false cast, let fly, and—pow!—a gust of wind tosses that dry fly two feet left of what you thought would be the perfect shot, just outside the fish's feeding lane. What do you do? If you're like most people, you want to give it another shot. You quickly load up and try again. Bad call.

"Live with it," said Missouri River guide Pete Cardinal, after that scene played out for us one afternoon. "If you make a bad cast, let your fly float out of that trout's range of vision, then go again, but *not* before." If you miss, even by a little bit, there's nothing wrong with letting the fly slide behind a trout before casting again. And more importantly, there's everything wrong with the whirling, splashing, slurping racket of a frustrated caster ripping a slightly off-target fly from the periphery of a feeding fish.

It takes practice and discipline, believe me. You make a mistake, and you want to try again. That's human nature. But there are no do-overs in trout fishing. The sooner you learn to accept what happened, good or bad, and adapt your thinking to what might happen next, that's when you become a better angler. Watch that fish the next time. Rip it away, and the show's over. Let it ride, and you're still in business. —**K.D.**

61. Feeling Skitterish

The lesson was delivered by an old game warden on his home water, the Frying Pan River in western Colorado. Not one for frills, he never varied from his standard rig of two wet flies to tempt trout from the pocket water along the lower river.

This strategy seldom failed and, in any case, worked more often than what might be considered a more sophisticated approach. Often overlooked in the modern obsession with precise entomology, the ancient art of skittering wet flies along the surface remains as effective as during the days of Walton and Cotton.

Hungry trout seldom refuse a fly sliding along the surface, and this replication of something so patently alive also serves as a wake-up for fish that might be off their feed. One fly works well, two are better, and three, if you can keep them from tangling, are best of all for covering the most water. Happily, this tactic requires only short casts and can be used effectively in close quarters and on small streams where other presentations are difficult. —**C.M.**

62. Negatives into Positives

Faced with conflicting currents that make standard dead-drift nymph presentations problematical, consider making that contrary flow your friend. Simply turn around and quarter your cast downstream, allowing the tricky currents to help manipulate your fly in an enticing manner rather than struggling to achieve an effective drift in the other direction.

The notion is to make your fly imitate a struggling organism or an insect emerging to the surface. Here's the drill: Use a split shot or comparable weight to sink the fly, then bring it to the surface by raising the rod tip. You'll both feel and sense the strike, which may also come at the end of the drift when the fly is hanging near the surface.

The Western Coachman is a favored fly for this technique, as are the Prince nymph and various caddis emerger patterns. This is also an effective method for traditional wet fly patterns. —**C.M.**

63. When in Doubt (Set the Hook)

Always curious about the mysteries of trout fly fishing, Jack Dennis took an underwater camera into a local stream to discover what really happens when anglers made presentations to fish beneath the surface.

Among his more revealing discoveries: Anglers failed to detect 40 percent of the strikes they received using conventional nymphing techniques, particularly with indicators.

The reason? Invariably, the problem was too much slack in the line. Dennis found that fish feeding actively on a plentitude of insects floating past their noses seldom moved much; rather, they simply held their position and opened and closed their mouths. In such situations, anglers generally failed to realize when a trout had taken the artificial fly.

In feeding situations with fewer insects, when trout drifted up or darted sideways to take the artificial, the line often moved sufficiently for the angler to detect the strike.

One solution to a light bite is to get as close as possible to the fish, eliminating as much loose line as possible. But the ultimate cure for missed strikes is keen concentration, setting the hook at the slightest pause in the drift. Make the hook set quick and short, keeping the fly down in the target area if you don't connect. —**C.M.**

64. No Clear Indication

The decision to use a strike indicator for nymphing is usually a matter of preference rather than necessity. You can catch fish either with or without an indicator, whether it's a balsa bobber, piece of yarn, or a large buoyant fly.

Success generally depends upon conditions. Short-line nymphing without an indicator often works best in a swift, deep run where you can get close to the trout. Often, you'll feel the strike directly and quickly, an advantage over the delay caused by slack line common with indicators.

On the other hand, an indicator helps deliver a good presentation at a greater distance and offers a good visual for those who need or desire it. Should you choose an indicator, select a system that allows for quick depth adjustment, a critical element in presenting the fly in different locations as you move along the stream. Reluctance to change depths may be the most important reason for nymphing failure.

One variable is beyond dispute: In a strong wind, get rid of the indicator. It's like trying to cast a kite, plus it catches the wind when on the water, accelerating the speed of the drift. —**C.M.**

65. First Impressions

In a similar vein, the first cast to a feeding trout, either at or beneath the surface, is by far the most important. Make the proper presentation right off the bat and your chances for a hookup skyrocket. Show the wrong fly or miss the mark with the cast or drift and you'll likely put the fish on alert that something is amiss. You have only one chance to make a good first impression. Take pains to make that shot count. —**C.M.**

66. Ready, Set, Go

To avoid needlessly spooking fish, make all your tackle preparation before you move into position to cast. That way, you'll spend less time in a place where you're likely to be seen, particularly by trout that might be moving about.

By remaining a few yards away from the point of attack, you're also more likely to observe a feeding fish or some other indication of where best to begin. —**C.M.**

67. Dress for Success

Drab clothing that blends well with the background is important when approaching trout: greens in forests or tall grass, tans and browns when the backdrop turns dull. Avoid contrasting colors such as white, yellow, or red. Whatever you choose, it also helps to keep a low profile when making a close approach. —**C.M.**

68. Watch That Line

When nymphing without an indicator, concentrate on the visible bit of line or leader that is farthest away, the last thing you can see down in the water. This object should become your strike guide, the thing that provides the quickest indication that a fish may have taken the fly. If that spot on the line stops or moves in any way contrary to drift, set the hook. —**C.M.**

69. When Shorter Is Better

With a sinking line, shorten the leader to about three feet. The whole purpose of using a sinking line is to get the fly deep. A long leader causes the fly to ride up out of the zone, or at least take a long time getting there. You'll seldom spook trout. To quote Lefty Kreh, "Fish don't swim up your line to see how long your leader is." —**C.M.**

70. **Don't Be a Slacker**

When casting upstream, slack in the fly line as it drifts back toward the angler becomes an enemy on two counts: it catches current, accelerating the natural drift of the fly, and it creates a time lag when setting the hook, causing missed strikes.

Successful anglers take pains to retrieve loose line, but never so fast as to advance the fly. To take up slack quickly, pin the line beneath the index finger holding the rod grip. Grasp the line behind that finger and strip briskly to recover slack before it accumulates. —C.M.

71. **A Hitch in Time**

Trout spend more time in swift, shallow water than we might imagine—particularly when oxygen is scarce during summer heat. The challenge of catching them lies in making a good presentation in difficult currents; the solution comes from making this condition work for you through a device called the riffle hitch.

To do this, throw a half-hitch onto the side of a small streamer or hopper a quarter inch or so behind the eye of the hook—always on the side of the fly nearest you as you look downstream. Experiment with the hitch placement until you find the proper balance with each fly. With a quartering cast downstream, the fly skitters across the surface in a way that excites trout to vicious strikes. —C.M.

72. **Spiderman Rules**

When trout turn lethargic, it's time for a wake-up call. Lee Wulff's favorite alarm bell was a spider skated across the surface of a pool. There's something about a wispy pattern performing a delicate ballet across the water that fish seem unable to resist. Even if it doesn't move fish, just performing this maneuver will keep you entertained for a while. —**C.M.**

73. **Night Moves**

Smart fishermen know that the best action often occurs when most other anglers are eating, drinking, and sleeping. Lacking eyelids, all fish prefer periods of low light. This is particularly true of reclusive species such as brown trout. If you want to catch more and bigger fish, try fishing very early and late, even at night when conditions are right.

Older, larger trout, in particular, have a natural aversion to light and the human activity that comes with it. The size of your catch generally will be in inverse proportion to the degree of daylight.

The first thing you achieve with this strategy is to get rid of nearly all the other fishermen. Places that might have been crowded earlier in the day now fairly ooze tranquility. Trout that may have remained hunkered down against the onslaught will now venture out to feed aggressively.

On still water, larger trout feel more at ease near the surface, both from the standpoint of temperature and safety. You'll now find them prowling the shoreline shallows in search of a meal, well in range of your casts. Stream fish more readily accept large, bushy flies on the surface; violent strikes are easy to detect, even in the dark. —**C.M.**

74. The Refusal Rise: What the Fish Said

Some of life's best lessons are learned through adversity—such as the times when a nice trout bulges right beneath your fly but doesn't eat it. Behind every rejection, there's usually a message.

More likely than not, the fish is saying your fly is too big. If you're watching the hatch closely, you've probably got the insect and color right. But you may have overlooked size, almost always the most important element in matching a hatch.

Unless you're dealing with hoppers or some other big terrestrial, trout generally are less suspicious of a small fly than a large one. When you get that kind of refusal, you know the trout is interested, but something isn't quite right. One false rise may be an anomaly. Get two and you'd better take action.
—C.M.

75. A Hanging Offense

The place: a deep pool on a western river where the water below the dam has slowed to a trickle.

The hour: 0-dark-30.

The situation: large rainbow trout rolling noisily where the trickle enters the pool.

The problem: after just two casts with a Woolly Bugger, all feeding stops, every fish put down.

The solution: the inadvertent discovery that these trout will take a hanging fly, one waving in the current with no retrieve motion at all.

Our perplexed angler left the fly dangling in the slack flow while pawing through his fly box for a replacement. Suddenly, the line went screaming off into the darkness with a big fish attached. After fighting the big bow, our angler patiently repeats the procedure and is rewarded with another jarring strike.

Three rainbows later, the reality has sunk in. The trout were frightened by the moving streamer. It's time to slow down. Let the fly wave naturally in the current, forming the silhouette of a small baitfish while allowing the natural movement of the materials to do the work. —**C.M.**

76. A Cure for Nymphing Neurosis

Here's yet another pitch for the value of an additional split shot or two. Imagine this scenario. You're casting to fish feeding on nymphs near the bottom, but you can't buy a bite. Either you're using the wrong fly or not making the proper presentation.

Which is it? You keep changing patterns, but you've got the nagging suspicion that the problem lies with your drift. What's to do? Most veteran anglers start by ensuring they have enough weight on the line to get the nymph down to where the fish are likely to be.

After you've satisfied that basic requirement, then proceed with the fly-juggling act with far more assurance that the puzzle can be solved. —**C.M.**

77. **Staying Humble**

You can spot an angler who is proficient on quiet meadow streams by the wear showing on the knees of his waders, as keeping a low profile is often the difference between spooking fish in slack currents or not.

Try casting from your knees, keeping the rod tip low as possible. Crawl into an approach position if you must. —**C.M.**

78. **Sunny Side Down**

Lacking eyelids, trout don't like looking into the sun. Make your approach with the sun at your back, particularly early and late in the day, and you'll get closer without being seen; plus, you'll also be better able to spot the fish. A bonus is that you'll

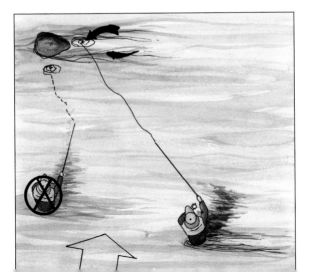

eliminate a lot of those light flashes from the glossy finish of your rod and all those shiny objects dangling from your vest.

That said, the spoilers can be shadows. Put the sun behind you, but be mindful of the shadows you cast onto the run. A few steps to the right or left can make a huge difference.—**C.M.**

79. Look Beyond Your Indicator

Whether plastic, balsa, or yarn, indicators are effective and popular tools for many nymphing situations. Many anglers have come to depend upon them. Trouble is, the considerable delay between the time a trout actually takes a fly and when the signal is telegraphed up the leader to the indicator often results in missed fish.

If you use indicators, work on your the ability to keep one eye on the bobber and the other on where you expect your fly to be. Watch for a flash or any other movement that might suggest a fish has taken your fly. Your percentage of hook-ups will skyrocket.—**C.M.**

80. The Down-Current Hook-Set

As a guide, I often see people make great casts and drifts, then yank the fly out of a trout's mouth when it hits. The problem is that they try to set the hook in an upstream direction.

Trout face into the current 99.9 percent of the time. They eat things that float toward them. If a trout eats a bug (dry fly or nymph) that is floating toward it, why on earth would you think it's a good thing to rip that fly back upstream? The whole point of fly fishing is to set that J-shaped hook into the trout's

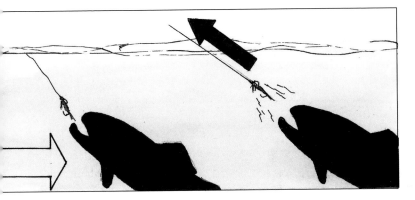

mouth, and that can only happen if you set the hook down-current (not downstream ... *down-current*).

It seems as if our instinct tells us to lift, flick, and pull upstream with every take. Before you make your next cast, take a minute, watch the way the current is moving, and then plan to set the hook down-current in the same direction of the current flow. This will increase your success-to-net ratio tenfold.
—**K.D.**

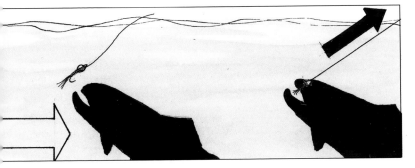

81. **Where the Trout Are**

You're fishing a dry fly on a smooth-flowing stream. You see the rise ring of a feeding trout and are ready to make your cast. At this point, it's vital to understand just where the fish really is and where you should place your fly. To make this judgment, you need to understand a trout's economy of motion as it pertains to hydraulics.

Unless chasing a fast-moving meal, trout never hurry. In life's game of calories gained versus energy expended, slow and steady is the rule.

The rhythm works something like this: When a trout sees an insect entering its window of vision, it tips its body upward, allowing the current to lift it to the surface and slightly backward, much like a kite in the wind. This means the point at which a trout meets the fly generally is slightly downstream from its original holding lie, distance depending upon speed of current. Following the take, the fish swims back to the comfort of its original watch point beneath the surface.

To place the fly properly, you'll need to calculate this holding place, then cast just upstream from the window to achieve the same presentation as the naturals in the drift. Your fly must land a yard, perhaps more, upstream from where you saw the rise ring.

Once you learn the riddle of distance and rhythm, you'll start catching more fish. —**K.D.**

82. **That Vision Thing**

To gauge how to best present fake food to trout, it's important to know how and what they see. The same basic understanding is also vital when trying to approach a fish without being sighted.

Books have been written on the subject. In this brief context, it's enough to know that trout view the world out and upward through a cone-shaped window—very narrow at the eye of the fish and progressively broader with the distance to the surface.

For a trout holding six feet beneath the surface, the oval window is much larger than at three feet, and so on. To a trout sipping floating mayflies from a watch point a foot beneath the surface, the window is quite small. Place your fly in a drift that brings it inside this window and you'll probably get a rise; outside, nothing. Precise presentation is paramount for rising trout. —**C.M.**

83. Timing the Rise

While considering placement of a fly so a trout can see it, an angler must take into account the element of casting to a fish rising in a regular rhythm to naturals. This is where timing comes in. The process described earlier, in which a trout lifts to eat an insect and then returns to its station, requires a brief period of time, perhaps three or four seconds. During a dense hatch, with lots of insects available in the drift, it's relatively easy to note the shortest of these intervals and gauge your presentation accordingly.

If you rush the cast, your fly will appear before the trout is ready, perhaps providing an awkward view as it slides past, causing alarm. Wait too long and the trout likely will have taken a natural instead, causing you to repeat the process—with a greater chance that you'll spook the fish.

Particularly with fish that receive lots of pressure, it's important to make your first presentation a good one. Take a moment to survey the situation. Gauge the rhythm to get timing right.
—**C.M.**

84. Be a Sneak

Knowing what a trout can see affects the way we approach them. Since trout have a blind spot to the rear, an approach from downstream is generally best. There are other considerations, however. The cone of vision, as it pertains to the angle of refraction of light, means that it's sometimes easier to approach a trout holding in very shallow water, or near the surface.

This is true only up to a point. The variable comes when an angler is guilty of heavy footfalls along shore or making waves or splashing when wading. Trout near the surface are particularly sensitive to vibration, while those in deeper or turbulent water much less so. A shallow fish may not see you, but it can sense your presence from a considerable distance. Approach with caution.

An angler can remove himself from a trout's area of vision by reducing his height. For example, a fisherman wading waist deep or crouching from his knees becomes half as tall. With a stealthy approach, he can shorten the distance of his cast and make a more accurate presentation. Conversely, an angler casting from a high bank should expect to make much longer casts to avoid being seen. —C.M.

85. Off Broadway

When casting to a fish that's visible near the surface on a sunny day, be aware that the shadow from your line will cause it to spook. To prevent this, direct false casts away from the fish and on the opposite side from the sun. Only when you get the distance right and are ready for the presentation should you then cast toward the trout. —**C.M.**

86. Downstream and Dirty

One way to avoid "lining" a fish with your cast, as well as a cure for tricky currents and difficult drifts, is to make your presentation directly downstream. Simply place your offering in the line of drift above the fish and let the current do the rest. The first thing the trout will see is your fly, not your line.

It's not always simple, of course. You'll need to stay far enough upstream to avoid the window of vision. It also helps to use a presentation such as the "S" cast to keep slack in the line and to pay out line smoothly through the guides to extend the drift. —**C.M.**

87. How Dry Am I?

Keeping dry is desirable in martinis and rainstorms. When it comes to fishing a floating fly, it's critical. For reasons best known to trout, a fly that sinks ever-so-slightly when fish are feeding exclusively on the surface is refused consistently. Ours not to wonder why, ours just to keep it dry.

The fly-fishing industry has created various liquid, paste, and crystal products to keep flies dry. With use, you'll discover what works best for you. Just remember that you have to keep applying the stuff regularly to get its benefits.

Perhaps the best strategy is to change flies often, particularly after catching a fish. Allow the used fly to dry completely before treating it again. Sometimes the fault is in the fly itself, either through poor design or improper material. If you find this fly in your box, throw it out.

Anglers are schooled to pay close attention to speed of the drift, but lose sight of the precise fashion in which their fly floats. The latter is as important as the first. —**C.M.**

88. Getting to the Bottom of Things

The month: January. The river: Colorado's Roaring Fork. The challenge: getting flies down to sluggish trout holding close to the bottom in extremely cold water. Three anglers tried a more conventional approach, drifting bead-head nymphs with a couple of split shot while furiously mending line to neutralize a steady current. Each caught an occasional fish, working hard for their strikes. A fourth companion seemed to have a trout with every second cast, chortling at the obvious discomfort of his far-less-successful friends. Closer inspection revealed his novel and highly effective approach. His flies were heavily weighted with tungsten wire and a tungsten bead, with about the same specific gravity as a ship's anchor. He also pinched two larger split shot to his leader. The truly novel ingredient was the balsa indicator, much like an antique panfish bobber, that was large enough to stay afloat above all that weight. With this rig, our friend kept his offering dead-drifted in the zone much longer than anyone else, and he had the fish to show for it.

Such a weighty assembly isn't for everyone, but when trout are hugging bottom, it gets results. —C.M.

89. Time on Water Equals Fish, Part I

I distinctly remember one spring afternoon on the Green River in Utah, fishing from Denny Breer's boat. We were well downstream from the Flaming Gorge Dam, in the "C" section, far from the weekend crowds upstream. The water was clear, yet large trout were keyed on big dry cicada patterns (this is why you go to fish the Green River).

I made a shot against the bank as the boat floated downstream, and after a few seconds lifted the rod tip to fire away

at a riffle behind a rock. "No . . . hang on! Wait," said Denny. "Let that fly ride a while. Mend, keep it drifting, but keep it in the water. If it's not in the water for at least 30 seconds, that's not long enough." As if on cue, a brown trout emerged from the river bottom, then lollygagged its way downstream, nosing the back of my fly (almost like it was sniffing it) for a good 30 yards as we drifted along. Finally, almost painstakingly, the trout wrapped his choppers around the bug with deliberation, and I set the hook.

It turned out to be the biggest fish I caught (or have since caught) on the Green River. We often hear the adage that flies in the air have never caught a trout, and it's so true. Too much casting can be a bad thing. But flies in the water, especially when they are set up right and floating through feeding lanes, are never a bad thing. Fishing from a drift boat allows you to keep those flies on the water longer, which is why you do it. Set them up correctly, then let them ride for as long as they float, and for as long as you can manage them.

After all, explained Denny, "Time on water equals fish." Keep that in mind wherever you fish, whether you're in a boat or not. —**K.D.**

90. **Time on Water Equals Fish, Part II**

The "Time on Water Equals Fish" axiom has a dual purpose. Pertaining to the angler, there is simply no substitute for experience. No book, magazine or newspaper article, video or DVD can ever take the place of the hands-on learning value of actually being on the trout river, soaking it all in, and seeing how this game unfolds firsthand. Reference resources can be helpful primers, and good ones can shorten the learning curve dramatically.

But in the end, fly fishing for trout becomes an innate endeavor. You develop instincts. You learn to know where to look for trout. You learn to cast as a reflex reaction. You sense a trout's presence. You anticipate a strike before it happens. You recognize the slightest motions and telltales. You know where a trout will turn during a fight. In the end, this doesn't have real impact until you see it and experience it for yourself. You will ultimately be your own best coach after a long period of trial, error, and experience.

Terry Gunn, owner of Lees Ferry Anglers Fly Shop and Guide Service, on the west side of the Colorado River in Marble Canyon, Arizona, once told me that an angler doesn't get really good until he learns how to teach himself, and realizes that he is doing it. It might seem like a long way off, but it happens to everyone who sticks with this game. Sooner or later, the game shifts from the mind to the gut. And you'll catch more fish.

The key is to spend your time reinforcing good habits and techniques. Spend your time wisely. Squander your experiences by replaying bad habits, and you'll never get much better. But improve in incremental bites, every time you hit the water, and success will become second nature. Time on water equals fish.
—K.D.

91. Switch Bugs on an Obvious Refusal

August on the Henry's Fork (the graduate school of fly fishing) can be cruel. Hatches are sparse and, on hot days, your best chances for trout in the vaunted Railroad Ranch section often

revolve around throwing hoppers and other terrestrial patterns ("Indian jewelry," as author/angler René Harrop described them one evening, over beers at the A-Bar in Last Chance, Idaho).

Nevertheless, I found myself pressing forward one morning with guide Bob Lamm. We spotted a riser on the bank, and I let the cast fly. It was a good shot, well in front of the fish, with no drag on the fly. We saw the fish poke his nose toward the bug, then plunge back into the depths behind a rock. I loaded up to fire another cast. "Hold on . . . wait!" Bob said, literally grabbing the rod during my backcast. "He didn't like that fly the first time, on a good cast. What makes you think he's going to change his mind?"

So we paused, and Bob reached into his fly box for a slightly different hopper pattern. He tied it on, and as he did so, the fish rose again. "Now try him," Bob said. Same cast, same drift, and this time that fish chewed it up. We hooked and landed him.

It's a natural reaction to want to try again after you've just missed a big fish, but the point is that you need to make a slight adjustment, especially if you did everything right the first time. In those cases, change the offering. Tom Whitley, a great guide in the Denver area, says he changes his fly pattern down a size after an obvious refusal. Don't show them the same thing, the same way. Adjust. Trick the trout. That's what this game is all about, isn't it? —**K.D.**

92. One at a Time

Here's a common scenario that leaves most anglers scratching their heads in frustration, at one point or another. You're in a classic dry fly run, and it seems as if 100 trout are gulping away at insects on the surface.

You make a cast in one direction but wait, there's another one; lift, swish, land the fly. He's gone, but there's one! Cast again, and you're doing it all wrong. Scatter-shoot your casts in a pod of rising fish, and you are effectively being everywhere and nowhere. Pick one target, and stay on it, preferably moving from the back of the school forward. If you're good, you can pick them off one at a time.

The trout won't notice anything that's happening behind them, but they will notice everything happening in front of them. Lock onto a target, be patient, time your cast, and go. As Terry Gunn once told me, casting at a pod of rising fish is like shooting into a flock of quail with a shotgun; you'll inevitably miss them all. Pick one, measure your shot, and squeeze the trigger.

You might get lucky when you flock shoot, but for the most part you're only busting sky. In the case of trout fishing, if you get wild with your casts and don't focus on one fish, you'll only add to your frustration by losing the whole opportunity. Everywhere gets you nowhere. —**K.D.**

93. Stack Mending for Drifts

As long as your flies are floating naturally, and the drift is good, there's no rule against making multiple mends to cover lots of water. In fact, in big rivers, like the Colorado at Lees Ferry in Arizona, and up on Oregon's Deschutes, stack mending for long drifts is a smart way to fish.

Make your cast, let your flies settle, then make your mend. As the flies float downstream, make another mend, feeding more line as you go. Then another. And another. Mete out line gently by wiggling the rod tip to feed line through the guides; at the same time, don't get caught with so much slack that you cannot set the hook when your indicator stalls 50 or 60 feet away from you. It can be tricky. The key is making many small, gentle mends as you feed your line through the run. —**K.D.**

94. Fish Flies Atypically

Don't be married to the notion that you have to fish every fly exactly the way it's designed. For example, one of the best nymph fishing afternoons I ever enjoyed was with Tony

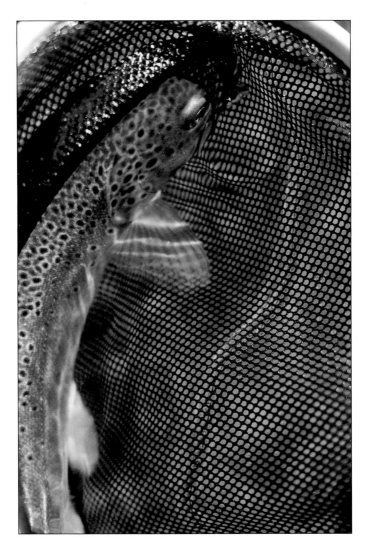

Fotopulos on the Colorado River. Our magic bug? A Dave's Hopper. That pattern is meant to be fished dry, but that wasn't working. What did work was letting the bug get waterlogged, then fishing it like a nymph through the deep holes.

That might not be a classic presentation. But ask yourself, do grasshoppers drown in heavy currents? Then ask, if you were a big ol' brown trout and you saw that juicy meal floating by, would you take a bite? —**K.D.**

95. Shake, Shake, Shake (Your Streamer)

If lethargic trout seem unwilling to take that final lunge for your streamer, try this wake-up call. When your fly enters a likely zone, give the rod tip a vigorous up-and-down shake. The pulsing action this delivers to the fly will often make a trout respond. —**C.M.**

96. Snake Your Way to Success

Most casting instructors call it the "S" pickup. Perhaps a more graphic way to think of this technique of reducing surface disturbance when lifting the line from the water is to imagine the motion a snake makes while swimming. However you picture it, this method lifts the line in smooth segments rather than ripping it from the surface in a way that spooks trout.

It works this way: Strip in loose line, then initiate the backcast by slowly and smoothly lifting the rod tip in a progressive squiggly motion. When the tip reaches approximately ten o'clock, apply the normal power stroke and resume regular casting.

Trout are extremely sensitive to surface commotion, particularly in calm water, and a rough, noisy pickup can spook every fish in a pool. Practice this tactic on a park pond until it becomes second nature. —C.M.

97. Ditch the Bobber

With the popularization of strike indicators, we've come to rely upon them too much, particularly in certain situations, such as in relatively shallow water. Trout that have been pressured often become indicator-shy and shift to the side when this rig drifts past. Be aware of this behavior and don't hesitate to switch back to the technique we all used before the bobber craze began: a tight-line drift that involves using vision and feel to detect a strike. When dealing with spooky fish, be ready to go bobberless. —C.M.

98. More on Indicators

The solution to the previous problem is often as simple as switching to a smaller indicator. Use nothing larger than what you need to support the weight. Small indicators respond better to more subtle takes, allowing you to detect, and catch, more fish. Did we mention they're also easier to cast? —C.M.

99. Balloon Going Up

Among the most useful recent inventions is the round, soft-plastic indicator shaped like a small balloon. Two features make this a good choice: superior flotation for its size and ease in adjustment. Using a half-hitch knot slipped through the eyelet loop, it takes only a few seconds to adjust for depth or switch to a larger or smaller unit. Add two more reasons for choosing this indicator: It's less wind-resistant than yarn, thus easier to cast, and it requires no time-consuming dressing. —**C.M.**

100. The Sting

A few years back, noted angler Frank Smethurst and his partner Gifford Maytham won $40,000 on one of those made-for-TV competitions with the simple trick of tying a tiny trailer hook, often called a stinger, very close behind a larger fly. They'd noted trout striking short on what turned out to be a difficult day of catching. The stinger was virtually concealed by the main fly. When spooky trout nipped at the back of the fly, they got a hook in the lip, and our intrepid anglers went home with a big payoff. —**C.M.**

101. Easy on the Grease

Whether or not to grease one's leader remains a subject of keen debate. Recent advances in subsurface photography offer clues to a solution. A greased leader coiled on the surface collects globs of light that warn fish. At the same time, a sunken leader tends to drag the fly down on pickup, necessitating frequent fly dressing. As a compromise, try greasing most of the leader while leaving the final 18 inches of tippet clean. This part should sink slightly, making it more difficult for a trout to see. —**C.M.**

102. **Accuracy Above All**

When contemplating the narrow cone of vision of a trout that's surface feeding in relatively shallow water, two things stand out. One is that a cautious angler can approach to a close position, particularly from behind. But this advantage also comes with a challenge. This narrow window dictates that the fly be presented precisely in the trout's line of drift—no more than a foot or so to either side and just above the edge of the window. So there you have it: cautious approach, close to the target, short, accurate cast, trout on the line. Any questions? —**C.M.**

103. **Beware the Wave**

Most anglers get it when it comes to avoiding the thumping and splashing of clumsy wading, but we often forget about that little bow wave of water we push ahead of us as we move into the pool. These rings, sent out one leg after the other as we slowly wade, can create a pulsing light, particularly on sunny days, that can spook any nearby trout. Depending upon the depth and character of the current, it's often best to not enter

the water at all. Trout frequently lie in the soft water near shore. Try to pick those off first, then move into the pool. —**C.M.**

104. Spare the Rod

It may seem sacrilege to think ill of an object for which we spent a king's ransom, keep cloistered in a velvet case, and flash to our friends at every opportunity. The key word here is *flash*, as in the sheen that sparkles from this graphite marvel when waved in sunlight. Awareness of this flare is important both in approaching and casting to a fish. Keep the rod low on approach and be aware of the sun's position during the cast. Rod flash might help explain why we often have better success on overcast days. And it also might make us think about that ultra glossy finish the next time we buy a rod. —**C.M.**

105. Ups and Downs

Whether to present a fly up- or downstream is usually a matter of choice, but certain situations should be considered. Since trout generally face upstream, approaches from above must be stealthy and casts made from farther away. Hook sets from above tend to pull the fly from the fish's mouth, and pickups are more likely to frighten fish.

On the other hand, a downstream drift may be the only way to reach a difficult fish rising beneath an obstruction. A plus is that the fly becomes the first object that appears in the fish's window, a major advantage when addressing leader-shy fish. —**C.M.**

PART THREE

Reading Water: 37 Tips to Help You Find Trout in a River and Effectively Cast to Them

There are many reasons people gravitate to fly fishing. Some pick it up from a parent or relative. Others might try it by chance, and find themselves hooked. Perhaps a friend talked you into spending a day on the river; maybe you read the book *A River Runs Through It*, or saw the movie; possibly you needed a relaxing hobby, and simply decided to give fly fishing a try. We all get here, from various starting points.

Those who stay in this sport stay for one reason: finding fish. That means matching wits with instinct. And that centers around the ability to read water.

It's the same basic reason why many golfers also like fly fishing, and why golf analogies work well in explaining the how-to aspects of fishing with the long rod. Fly fishing is a relaxation hobby for the type-A personality. It's a thinking person's sport, just like golf.

Consider this rationale: A golfer plays an 18-hole round. He or she spends roughly two seconds actually swinging various clubs (including the putter) to make each shot in a given round. Figure an average of five shots per hole for a decent golfer, times 18 holes, at two seconds a stroke; you're talking about three minutes of actual swing time over a four- or five-hour round of golf. The essence of that game is the mental aspect, everything that happens in-between club swings.

It's the same for the serious fly fisher. Yes, you're making false casts, and running drifts through runs to see what might happen. Even on a great day that might last hours, however, your actual fish fighting time will account for minutes, at best.

The real action takes place between the ears. Your eyes see subtle seams, current breaks, swirling pools, and you wonder where the fish are. Is one there, behind that rock? Maybe there's a fish up against the logjam. If I can get this fly to float in that riffle out in the current, *just so*, maybe . . .

The more time you spend understanding rivers, and currents, and the habits of trout, the better your odds are of hooking fish. More important, the more time you spend focusing and tuning in on the subtleties of rivers, the more you ultimately become a bona-fide fly angler. —**K.D.**

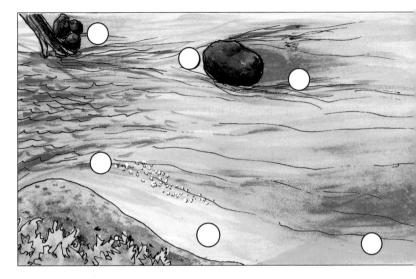

106. Fish Like Changes

The best lesson I ever learned about locating trout in a river came from a tuna captain. Fishing with Steve "Creature" Coulter, 40 miles off Hatteras, North Carolina, I stared out at the horizon and asked him how in the world he went about finding fish in the open ocean. "It isn't so hard," he said, smiling. "It's just like trout fishing."

For the record, Creature might be one of the most decorated big-game fishermen on the Atlantic seaboard, but his closet fishing passion is chasing trout with flies. "How do you figure that?" I asked, perplexed by the comparison.

"Fish like changes," he said. "Changes in currents, changes in depth, changes in water color, changes in structure. If you find a patch of sea grass floating in the open ocean, that's a structure change, and you'll find fish under it. If you find a place where currents converge, baitfish will school there and bigger fish will follow them. Reefs, wrecks, and rock formations attract fish too, as do underwater ridges and canyons."

Apply that thinking when you go to the trout river. Look for changes in currents, where swift water meets slow water; changes in structure, where rocks and trees create holding water; changes in depth, like shelves and pools; or changes in color, which usually signals a depth or structural transition.

"It's all pretty much the same," Creature told me. "You trout guys can walk or row a boat to find those changes, but you're essentially doing the same thing a tuna boat captain does in the ocean."

Find the changes, find the fish. —**K.D.**

107. **Depressing Advice**

The subject wasn't really personal hygiene, although it might have been for a wet-behind-the-gills angler grubbing his way along a series of Montana rivers in the early 1970s. Faced with the dual challenge of my first float trip and the mysteries of the lower Madison River, notorious as the "world's longest riffle" for its lack of distinguishing characteristics, I presented my dilemma to Lee Wulff.

Noted for his economy of speech, the legendary angler answered me with a single word: bathtubs. The wisdom of this odd advice soon became clear, however. In what appears to be an even-flowing river, look for holes in the surface. Cavities in the riverbed that form a resting place out of the main flow are echoed on the surface as slight depressions.

For an angler zipping along in a drift boat, the task lies in spotting these depressions well ahead, in time to prepare a suitable cast. You'll recognize them as low spots on the surface, a direct reflection of the bathtub effect immediately below. —**C.M.**

108. The Shadow Knows

Most trout are endowed with a natural camouflage, lovely variations of color tones and spots that makes them difficult to see. But no fish can hide its shadow. Veteran observers often look specifically for this giveaway rather than the actual fish, particularly against the contrasting background of a pale river bottom. —**C.M.**

109. Watch for the Flash

Despite their ability to hide effectively, there are times when trout completely betray their whereabouts. In particular, I'm talking about those times when they turn aggressively to intercept an emerging insect, particularly a fast-moving species such as caddis.

Watch the water closely and you'll eventually see what appears to be a flashbulb explosion, a sure sign that an aggressive trout has just turned its bright flank to take an insect. When the light goes on, this reveals not only the location of the fish, but a clue to what it may be eating.

When you see this in the vicinity of your drift, set the hook. The flash likely indicates a fish has taken your fly. —**C.M.**

110. You've Got to Pick a Pocket (or Two)

While searching for that big run that everyone figures will hold several trout, many anglers overlook smaller patches of holding water that, taken collectively, might prove even more productive. You'll find these pockets of soft water behind rocks or in overlooked places where subtle currents merge. The payoff comes in casting to trout that get less attention from other anglers, with less wasted time walking up and down the banks. —C.M.

111. Rock On

That rock in the middle of the river or jutting off the bank should always get your attention. Why? Because that slab of

granite affects the flow of the river, altering the current and creating subtle microcurrents around it. From downstream, you'll be able to see two distinct current lines to the right and left, where the water folds around the rock. Eventually, those currents merge like the bottom point of the letter "V." That's where cast number one should land, at the bottom of the "V."

Your next casts should be right up the two current seams. The fish will usually be where the fast water meets the slower water. That dead spot right behind the rock might also be worth a cast or two, although the fish usually don't tuck their noses right onto the stone.

Think about it. The food is washing downriver, packed into that seam where the current meets the slower water. The fish could swim out into the heavy water, but that takes energy, and the insects there are moving by at a quicker pace. If you were a fish, wouldn't you hang out where you have to use as little energy as possible to hold your position, especially when the buffet is churning right there? —**K.D.**

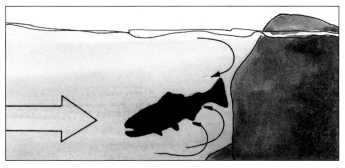

Pillow

112. Pillow Talk

Trout like hanging out behind rocks, but it's always worth looking in front of them as well. The hydraulic effects of water rushing downstream and pressing against a rock create a small backwave in front of the rock. Call it a cushion or pillow, but a smart (often big) trout can ride that wave just like a surfer on a board, expending little energy, and reaping the benefits of seeing and eating insects as they wash downstream.

Never leave a rock without at least making a cast or two on the front side. —**K.D.**

113. Rob the Banks

The Yellowstone River is one of the last great un-dammed waterways in the West, and in many anglers' opinions, the ultimate trout river. Fishing the Yellowstone with author and guide Kim Leighton for several days was a particularly enlightening experience, because he taught me the importance of adhering to the banks when targeting casts. Although the mighty Yellowstone is wider than a four-lane highway in some areas, it is amazing how much of the trout population can be found within feet, if not inches, of its banks.

The reason is simple: Trout find cover such as rocky outcroppings and fallen logs along the banks. They are less exposed to predators such as eagles and herons there, especially when compared to the open currents in the middle of the river. They also find plenty of natural forage, including sculpins and grasshoppers, close to the banks.

A trout angler should concentrate on "robbing" the banks. Whether fishing from a boat in a downstream direction, or wading upstream, your first focus should always be tight to the bank. Watch where you step. Fix your attention on the bank, and work your way out toward the middle of the river, covering the bank-outward as you cast and move. —**K.D.**

114. **Rosenbauer's Rules**

Perhaps nobody has written as thoroughly and thoughtfully on the topic of reading water as Tom Rosenbauer, marketing director for the Orvis Company and the author of *The Orvis Guide to Prospecting for Trout* and *Reading Trout Streams*, among many other titles. Having had the opportunity to fish with Tom several times (most memorably a blanket Hendrickson hatch on the Upper East Branch of the Delaware, as well as on some remote streams in Chile), I've always been impressed by his deliberate, methodical approach on the water. One always sees Tom's wheels turning well before he uncorks that first cast.

I once asked him what were the first things he looked for when he got knee-deep in a river.

"I don't stand knee-deep in the river," he said. "I stay as far away as I can and still be able to see the water. Fish are often right on the edges, especially if you are the first person up the bank in the morning."

Tom noted that, absent telltale rises, he often assumes that the biggest fish will be at the tail of a pool. He doesn't necessarily target his first cast there, however.

"If I think I can cast into the seam and the faster water without messing up the tailout, I'll often cast there first," he explained. "The fish tend to be easier targets in faster water, so that's usually a good place to start, checking to see if you have the right fly, and getting your confidence." —**K.D.**

115. **Be the Tree**

When standing on a bank surveying the scene, Tom Rosenbauer always makes the effort to have his silhouette blend in against a bush or a tree.

"If you're standing out there all alone, creating shadows and a silhouette that wouldn't naturally be there, it defeats the purpose," he said. "Make yourself part of the landscape when you stand on the bank and read the water, and you will inevitably see more. In fact, it's amazing what you can see in stupid-looking, shallow water if you take the time to blend in with a tree." —**K.D.**

116. **Nervous Water**

Bonefish guides are always looking for patches on the water with telltale ripples that reveal movement under the surface.

They call it "nervous water" or (in Mexico) "agua nierviosa." When fish move through shallow water in schools, they make a subtle disturbance that reveals their presence, even when their fins do not beak the surface.

This is also true with trout, especially in flat water like slow-moving spring creeks and lakes. It's always worth looking for nervous patches of surface water when you are figuring out where to make your first cast. —**K.D.**

117. Your Fly Rod Cannot See

Being able to cover a lot of water from a stationary spot in the river is an important attribute for any angler. Start short and cover those currents that look most appealing. Then you can make that tricky roll cast across the eddy. How about punching that long cast out into the main current? If you can hit all the targets from one spot, you're better off than most folks. The less you move, the more your odds improve, because trout are easily spooked by the noises of boots shuffling along the bottom and by splashes made by a fisherman in motion.

That said, it's important to pause and remember a simple lesson before you go spraying your casts all over the river. You see with your eyes, not your fly rod. Look before you start prospecting with casts. Every time. One or two well-conceived, well-planned casts are almost always more effective than 30 casts spread willy-nilly throughout a run.

Some anglers talk about "blind casting" as a way to cover water when they cannot actually see fish and there are no visible telltales to follow. That should be a last resort. There's always something to key on—a juicy current seam, a rock that creates a bucket of deep water in its wake—something!

Spend more time looking for something that will help you prioritize your casts, and less time blind casting without any real purpose. A smart quarterback doesn't throw the long bomb on every play. Neither should you. —**K.D.**

118. The Telltale Rise

An angler can often tell what type of fly to use by watching the rises of fish in a run. This is where the ability to read water directly influences fly selection. Learning to read water so you understand what insects fish probably are eating in a given stretch is the step that jumps an angler from Fly Fishing 101 straight into graduate school.

The slow, methodical rise and slurp with the nose of the trout visibly breaking the surface is a classic mayfly feed. When you see a fish porpoise, and the water being disturbed without a nose breaking the surface, you can figure the trout is likely picking off emergers just below the surface. A fast, splashy rise indicates that a fish is eating caddis swimming to the top. A super-subtle sip often suggests that the fish is keyed on midges. And a grasshopper take can be anything from a violent gulp to a long, laborious slurp; even a newbie will know that at first glance. —**K.D.**

119. Shadows in Bird Land

Trout are easily spooked by shadows moving overhead, but the stationary shadow is often an umbrella where they find comfort and calm, especially on bright, sunny days. The moving shadow above can trigger an instinctively defensive reaction; fish think it might be a predator. The stable shadow, one cast from an overhanging tree or a cut bank, gives the trout protection from such predators.

If you happen to walk up on a pool and spot some small trout, raise your arms or rod to create a shadow, and move the shadow above the fish. You'll see exactly what we're talking about: The fish will flee for cover almost instantly.

In the context of reading water, it's important to factor in the presence of shadows. The wind-blown tree branch that's waving back and forth above the river surface is not a good trout magnet. On the other hand, that tall rocky wall or stand of thick willows casting a shadow over the river is a good place to direct your attention.

Look for structure and current breaks in shadows when planning a cast. Absent these, cast near the dark-to-light shadow transition, usually a foot or two to the dark side.

Remember: stable shadows good, moving shadows bad.
—**K.D.**

120. Where Would You Be?

When reading water, ask yourself this simple question: *If I were a trout, where would I be?* Understand that your life revolves around three things: eating, not being eaten, and making little fish.

In the context of fly angling, the eating part is most important. Playing the role of trout, you understand that you primarily eat insects and smaller fish. You know that you'll find more

of both closer to the banks, so that's a good starting point to choose where you want to hang out in the river.

The insects you eat come in all forms: nymphs, emergers, adult bugs hatching, adult spinners falling to the surface to lay eggs, terrestrials falling into the river, and so forth. You know that mayflies, for example, like to lay eggs on gravel bottoms, and that that is where nymphs, emergers, duns, and spinners are likely to concentrate.

Currents also concentrate insects. Bugs get trapped and collected in the seam where fast water bumps up against slow water, for example. You (the trout) want to be near that seam, in a place where you aren't expending more calories to swim than you can consume.

At the same time, you don't want to become calories for another predator. You want to find cover in those rocks or under that log. Lacking thick cover, my exit strategy is to go to deep water. There has to be a place where I can escape to the depths when I'm threatened.

Making little fish is another matter. We spawn on gravel. Hopefully the angler reading this book won't mess with me when I'm on a spawning bed.

The more you ask yourself, "If I were a trout, where would I be?" while you are on the water, fishing, the easier reading water becomes. Thinking like a fish will make places and targets pop out before you cast. You'll overlook fewer targets, and catch more trout. —**K.D.**

121. The Five-step Run

When I'm reading water and approaching a run in a river, I like to use a five-step approach. Say there's a rock creating the run against a bank; a current seam sweeps outside the run, and an eddy forms inside toward the bank. How do you plan your casts?

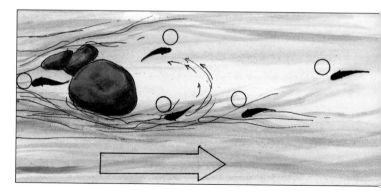

If you're like most anglers, you'd like to catch two or three fish out of this run, so step one is to cast to the tailout of the seam. You'll often find the biggest fish here. Be cautious and deliberate; shallow, slower water tends to make fish—especially larger, older fish—more skittish and selective.

Step two and three are casts following the seam upstream, toward the rock. Odds are the biggest fish in the run is somewhere in this area if he isn't at the tailout.

Another place the big boy might be is in the eddy, likely feeding against the current, facing downstream. That's my step-four cast, into the eddy, paying out line back toward the rock as the eddy sucks it upstream.

Step five is a well-placed cast or two on the cushion in front of the rock. Always fish the front of the rock and the front of the run. —**K.D.**

122. The Reverse Eddy

True or false? Trout always face upstream in rivers.

The answer: false.

Trout usually face up-*current* in rivers (though not always), and as currents inevitably mix and swirl under myriad influences that shape water directions (banks, rocks, timber, and so on), it's common to find trout facing downstream, feeding into that current.

The classic example of this is the river eddy: water washes around a giant rock or a gravel bar with such force that it creates a vortex, where water is spun around in reverse. These eddies are often prime spots for holding big trout, especially when mayflies, midges, and caddis are present, either nymphs or adults.

When reading water and assessing a run, always look for an eddy first. You know that main seam is there, and you know how to fish that, but spend a few minutes before that first cast by taking a long, hard look for an eddy.

The first telltale is watching the pattern of bubbles, twigs, leaves, and other flotsam on the surface. Insects on the surface are, of course, the best sign of all.

If you see the patterns of a reverse eddy in place, assume there are fish in it, and the reason those fish would be there is to eat.

The best cast to cover an eddy is a snake cast, where you leave slack at the end of your line, and gently feed that slack into the eddy as your flies drift upstream.

It's an extremely technical maneuver, but it can be very exciting, as you'll see and feel strikes much more effectively in the relative calm of an eddy. —**K.D.**

123. The Cut Bank

There is no place a big cutthroat or brown likes to hang out more than under a cut bank, where the high water currents of the river have scoured out a cave to hide in. Rainbows tend to prefer riffles and seams, although they, too, will inhabit cuts if there is enough current. When you find a horseshoe bend on the trout stream, which creates a deep, dark, cut bank, you can almost bet there will be a big brown trout living inside. Always be on the lookout for cut banks.

Once you've found your target, the trick becomes getting a fly to float into the strike zone. The overhang on a cut bank often makes dropping a shot directly in prime water

impossible. You can try to sidearm a cast, or skip a hopper into the cut, but that's sometimes too splashy to produce good results.

For me, the best approach for fishing the cut bank is from upstream, at an angle. I shoot the cast as tight to the bank as possible, then feed slack line and hope the current sucks the fly under the cut.

Make your first cast count. When fishing cut banks, your first presentation will typically be the one that gets hit. This isn't the place to experiment or mess around. —**K.D.**

124. **Low Water, High Water**

It's always easiest to read rivers during periods of low water. Natural features are more prominent, deep pools are more obvious (and important), and currents are clearly defined.

It's totally different when the water comes up. The currents are jumbled and more forceful, with dramatic breaks. *Everything* is deeper than normal.

But high water, for all its challenges, does give the angler a few hints. Heavy current usually pushes trout in one of two directions—to the bank or to the bottom, where they can find some hydrodynamic advantages that keep them sheltered.

When reading heavy water, key on color changes more than you would in other situations. The color tells you where submerged structure and dropoffs are located. —**K.D.**

125. Make Big Water Small

Most of us started fly fishing on small streams. They're easy to wade and easy to read. You have that one log sticking out

in the current, scouring the river bottom, and you can guess there's a good chance that Mr. Brown Trout might be hanging around it.

But what do you do when you get on a big, wide river, like the Madison, the Bighorn, the South Fork of the Snake, the Green, the Colorado, or the Delaware?

Among the guides I've fished with on these rivers, from Patty Reilly in Wyoming to Bob Lamm in Idaho to Joe Demalderis in New York, they all say that the key to reading them is to make big water small.

By that, they mean taking a river that's 50 yards wide and mentally dividing it into five 10-yard-wide sections. If you're wading upstream, start with the 10-yard section that's closest to the bank. Look for fish first. Now look for changes in structure—a rock, a log, a dropoff. Also look for changes in currents. Is there a spot where fast water meets slow water? Look for a depression in the bottom. If you've found the changes, make your casts: 10 casts, covering all the hotspots on your radar.

Nothing happened? Move out from the bank to the next 10-yard-wide section of water. Look for the same things—current breaks, structure, dropoffs—and cover them with solid casts.

Nothing happened? Move toward the middle and repeat the process. Do this until you can't wade any deeper (if you're wading big rivers, it usually is too deep to work all the way across), and until you feel you've made enough casts.

Next, wade upstream and start the process over. Make big water small in your mind. Divide and conquer, always working from the bank outward. —**K.D.**

126. What the Bass Boys Taught Me

It's funny how anglers like to embrace their own brand of fishing as high art and dismiss the others. Bass anglers may shun the fly rod as a buggy whip, while fly anglers may think of bass fishing as bubba fishing. Both are wrong. Fishing is fishing. Ultimately, what separates the contenders from the pretenders is the ability to read water, and that starts with understanding currents. Then know what the fish are eating, and how to present it to them. It's all essentially the same. The only difference is the stick used to make the cast, and that's not worth making a big deal over.

Having written about and fished with a number of bass pros, I'm always amazed to find out how many of them have at one point or another fly fished. In fact, I pick up some of my best fly-fishing ideas when I'm bass fishing with these guys.

Gary Klein, who has qualified for the Bassmaster Classic 28 times and is still rolling, credits fly fishing in part with his understanding of currents, structure, and how fish behave around them.

"Once you understand how moving water behaves, and creates currents, you learn where the fish concentrate in the water, and that's the same whether you're throwing crankbaits around a windblown point on a reservoir, or a dry fly in a river," said Klein. —**K.D.**

127. Everybody's Got to Be Somewhere

Rather than being discouraged by the rush of runoff, smart anglers realize that all raging water hasn't ruined their fishing opportunity. Instead, the action zone has simply been moved someplace else.

Most often, that someplace becomes the soft water formed by nooks and crannies near shore. You'll recognize them as slow backwaters or eddies behind rocks near the bank. During runoff, nearly every place where the current slows down markedly will hold trout.

To take advantage, an angler should be prepared to walk a good distance along the stream, skipping from one likely holding place to the next. This requires a certain amount of effort, but it does bring success at a time when there otherwise might be no fishing at all. —**C.M.**

128. Look Before You Leap—or Cast

In places with little angler traffic, trout often hold surprisingly close to shore. This is particularly true during the emergences of damselflies or stoneflies, two species that swim to land or to streamside objects on their way to becoming winged adults.

At other times, trout choose the shallows as a refuge from strong currents.

Most anglers make the mistake of casting across or wading through these places to reach more obvious holding places farther out in the stream. Take a few seconds to examine this close water for evidence of trout. —**C.M.**

129. A Breath of Fresh Air

When summer doldrums raise water temperatures, don't expect to find trout in the same deep pools they might have occupied earlier in the season. Warm water holds less oxygen, causing fish to seek those places where the mixing of air and water dramatically raises the percentage of dissolved oxygen.

At such times, look for them instead in fast-water riffles or below spills, especially during the hottest periods of the day. These white-water pockets may seem shallow or small, but they provide the essential element a trout needs to breathe. —**C.M.**

130. The Plot Thickens . . . or Not

Ever click on a suspense thriller well past the midway point and try to figure things out without peeking at the program guide? This happens to fly fishermen all the time. We arrive to the excitement of trout rising, but are puzzled by a complicated plot formed by more than one type of insect on the water—the equivalent of a clever director's ploy to complicate the story line. We also might guess the insect correctly, but miss the stage at which the activity is occurring.

With fly fishing, it's important to gather as many clues as possible before wading in. It helps to develop an understanding of insect behavior and trout rise forms. All this confusion can be eased by knowing the hatch schedule, so you can arrive ahead of time and catch the drama from the very beginning. Smart anglers put these timetables in their heads or even compile hatch charts for their favorite streams.

Think of this as the angler's version of the *TV Guide*. Tune in and you'll know much of the plot ahead of time. —**C.M.**

131. Downward Progression

No, this doesn't suggest the descending spiral of a good man gone bad. Rather, it's a plan for approaching a stream when you're not sure what the daily feeding pattern might be.

Considering that everyone loves to catch trout on dry flies, we start on the surface with a pattern that represents a prevalent insect. If this doesn't produce, descend to the next level with an emerger, a soft-hackle imitation of an insect in its ascent up through the middle depths toward the surface. Most consider this slightly less fun than dry-fly fishing, but still high on the scale.

Failing on both these strategies, a smart angler knows he has to hit bottom. When trout aren't responding higher up in the water column, chances are they're taking nymphs along the substructure. Time to add plenty of weight and tie on the larval form of the insect. Bottoms up. **—C.M.**

132. See Your Way Clearly

For many anglers, sight-fishing is the top-of-the-game approach, where the thrill of stalking and tricking their quarry is optimized as the drama unfolds in plain view. But there's a more utilitarian reason to make yourself a better sight-fisher. If you can see fish before you make a cast, you can dramatically increase your odds of hooking up. After all, knowing where fish are helps you pinpoint your presentations, recognize takes, and, ultimately, bumps your effectiveness to a much higher level.

"How in the world did you see *that*?" is a common refrain the best fishing guides often hear. While spotting fish may indeed

be an acquired talent, it doesn't require Superman vision or a carrot-rich diet to improve your acumen. If you follow these simple rules, you'll see your way to instant gratification on the water. . . .

Rule 1: The secret to spotting fish is knowing where to look. Sounds simple, but it's not. When I'm surveying a run in a trout river, for example, I know where fish typically like to hold—on the current seams, on cushions in front of rocks, in deeper depressions, against cut banks, and so on. When I try to spot fish, I'm pinpointing my gaze in those areas, one small section at a time. I might be fixed on a specific area, maybe six by eight feet, while you might be scanning a space the size of an Olympic swimming pool. If I don't see something in position A, I shift my attention to the next option. Divide and conquer, one small piece at a time.

Rule 2: Use sunlight to your advantage. When you're staring into sun glare, your vision is hampered; position yourself with the sun behind you, and it's like having a spotlight on the water (and the fish). Think about placing your body in relationship with your light source whenever possible, and you'll see more fish.

Rule 3: Focus on the subtle. Joe Demalderis, one of the best guides on the technical trout waters of the Delaware River system in New York and Pennsylvania, once told me, "You have to look for a single star, not the whole night sky." When you look only for the obvious, you minimize your effectiveness. Be suspicious of tiny reflections, shapes, and shadows that might reveal a fish. Remember, you aren't always looking for the whole fish; a tail or a nose is all you need to identify a target and direct that cast.

Rule 4: Learn to recognize and eliminate things that are *not* fish. Legendary redfish guide Chuck Naiser from Rockport, Texas, once explained to me that the sooner an angler can weed out mental distractions such as wind, ripples, waves, sticks, and bird shadows, the sooner he or she can get down to the business of identifying the position of feeding fish, and where to aim.

Rule 5: Let the water be your guide. On the bonefish and permit flats of Mexico's Ascension Bay, guide Alonso Choc of the Palometa Club makes his living by recognizing nervous water, where the motion of schooling fish reveals their locations. When you stare at a uniform water surface, and suddenly notice a disturbance, keep looking. The flashes and tails often follow in spots where you first see wakes or ripples.

Rule 6: Learn to look through water. Terry Gunn guides on the Colorado River in Lees Ferry, Arizona, possibly the best sight-fishing trout river in America. His secret to spotting fish is looking through the water column, as opposed to fixing gazes on the surface or the bottom. Doing so makes you more adept at noticing motion and subtle color changes that pinpoint a fish's location.

Rule 7: Take your time. When fish are feeding, oblivious to your presence, there's absolutely nothing wrong with taking an extra minute to survey the waterscape. Better to spend the time to acquire a legitimate target than to blind cast and drop a fly or bait on a fish's backside, thus ruining your chances.

Rule 8: Seek a vantage point and look into the current. If you're fishing a river, survey it from a high bank. In flat water, understand that there's a reason why guides pole skiffs from an elevated platform. Steelhead guide Tyler Palmerton of Oregon explains that, all things being equal, the key is to look up-current, because that usually positions you outside of a fish's peripheral vision and gives you a more detailed point of view.

Rule 9: Inconsistencies are the name of the game. Whether you're looking for bedded bass or trout holding in a run, you want to establish some waypoint markers in the water—rocks, weeds, depressions, and so forth. Colorado trout guide Jeremy Hyatt establishes a water template in his frame of view, and lets anything inconsistent with that template (color shades, shadows, motion) tip him off as to a fish's presence.

Rule 10: Wear polarized glasses. If I forget my waders at the start of the day, I'll usually improvise or tough it out. If I forget my polarized glasses, I'll go home and start fishing later. Good polarized eyewear is the foundation of the sight fishing game. Different frames and lenses offer various advantages, too. For example, on certain bright days, you might want amber or copper lenses, while in overcast conditions, yellow lenses might be better. The key is finding a style and model that wears so comfortably that you barely notice that you have them on. When you fish, your glasses should be an extension of your body. Without decent shades, you're almost fishing blind. —**K.D.**

133. Follow the Bubbles

One early morning, while dry fly fishing a trico hatch on Montana's Missouri River, guide Pete Cardinal checked me up, then told me to stop casting and watch the water. We were working a seam where fast water, colliding with a slow pool, was creating a foamy bubble line. At times, that bubble line would disperse

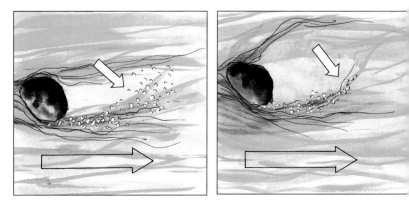

and spread out in wide fronds of white, wispy water. At other times, the currents converged and collected hatching insects in a tight, white highway that ran straight through the run. Until Pete pointed it out, I hadn't noticed that the fish were keyed into this system. When the currents dispersed or collapsed, the fish didn't rise. When the foam line formed a hard seam and collected those tiny mayflies, the trout began slurping away at the surface. The lesson? Follow the bubble line. When you see a pronounced foam or bubble line on the surface, there's a very good chance that trout will be underneath it, and feeding.
—**K.D.**

134. Raging Bull . . . You're Standing on Fish

A number of years ago, I did a short piece for *Field & Stream* on trout fishing guides and their favorite tactics and techniques. Their input was diverse, and everyone seemed to have a different point of view (which was perfect for the story). But when I asked them all about their number-one pet peeve, the answers were nearly uniform. "People don't look where they walk" . . . "People forget to look at the water right in front of them" . . . "Most folks forget to notice that some of the best trout are right near the bank." In other words, you're standing on your fish, stupid. Based on my own part-time guiding experiences, I have to agree, the absolute number-one frustration is to set up an angler in a good run, show him/her where to go and what to do, then go downstream to help a partner, then return to see him/her planted chest deep in the middle of where the fish . . . were.

Don't take anything for granted. By dashing out into the middle of a run, the only thing you guarantee is that any fish that were there will be gone. Look before you leap. Take your time. Who's wearing the stopwatch? Big Daddy might be tucked right under the bank in front of you, but you'll never know that if you barge right into the water like a raging bull. —**K.D.**

135. **Watch the Birdie**

Every bluewater angler worth his salt understands the message delivered by diving flocks of seabirds. Invariably, fish are feeding just below. Oddly, many freshwater fly fishers fail to capitalize on similar signs.

Let's start with an inviolate premise: Birds never lie. When you see swallows swooping low over the surface, be assured aquatic insects are about. The same applies to redwings or warblers flitting frantically in streamside bushes. Is the damselfly hatch in progress? Look for shorebirds grazing actively at water's edge.

Birds often respond to insect hatches ahead of trout. Take a hint from a feathered friend and you'll be ready with the right bug before the rise, adding precious minutes to that most exciting time of day. —**C.M.**

136. Trout Parts

Because trout are masters of camouflage, it's almost too much to expect to see an entire trout hanging like some picture in a book. Instead, look for pieces of the whole—the flutter of a fin, the soft waggle of a tail, the brief flash of a silver belly or, more subtly, the "little white blink" that nymph master G.E.M. Skues used to describe the opening and closing of the mouth of a trout taking nymphs. —**C.M.**

137. Seeing Is (Not) Believing

Among the most important, yet least understood, aspects of sight fishing is the role played by refraction. Put simply, the fish we think we see 20 feet away in shallow water will actually be closer and deeper than it appears. It will also seem larger than it really is, which may be where all those fish stories get started. —**C.M.**

138. Getting More from Glasses

Pay close attention to the odd-looking angler standing at streamside, the one nodding his head from side to side, maybe even rotating his glasses with his hands. He knows a secret about getting the most from his polarized glasses for seeing beneath the surface. By rotating the glasses slightly, they'll interface with another plane of light, opening up another window of vision into the water. —**C.M.**

139. Fish Furniture

From the perspective of comfort, think of rivers in much the same manner as your own living room. The baffle created by water striking a rock or abutment is like a soft pillow; the bolster of a midstream boulder is a comfortable easy chair; an extended weir becomes a sectional sofa, with resting spots at every turn. Think of a river in terms of comfort and many fish location problems will melt away. —**C.M.**

140. Fishing Lies

It's an old joke: Rainbow trout lie in fast water, brown trout lie in slow water, and fishermen lie almost anywhere, mostly in fishing shops. But there's truth in this. In a river dominated by rainbows, expect to find them in swift, open reaches with room to roam after insects. Biologists who use electro-surveys for census-taking swear they never find brown trout more than a couple feet from a rock. —**C.M.**

141. Worth Biting For

Armed with sharp teeth and a pugnacious attitude, brown trout tend to be territorial, willing to put up their fins to defend prize territory. Because of this, you can expect to find the best fish in the prime lies. And if a boss brown is removed from that lie, expect to find that position quickly claimed by another good fish. —**C.M.**

142. Love That Dirty Water

Don't be intimidated by dirty water. While it's easy to think that the fish won't be feeding because the water is off-color, that simply isn't the case.

Short of a full-on flood, fish are used to natural fluctuations in river levels, and they feed throughout all of them. They eat more often in certain conditions than others, but they do eat. Dirty water may be a problem for some anglers, but it isn't to the fish.

I'll take a day when the water is slightly stained over super-clear water any time, because that colored water tells me there's a lot of stuff (food) being washed into the river. That murkiness also camouflages me from the fish.

In dirty water conditions, avoid the area where a runoff-fueled creek is pumping thick, muddy water in the main current. Instead, look for the transition zone where dirty water meets clear (or at least clearer water), as that's a great place to cast.

If anything, dirty water narrows down the pockets of opportunity on a river. There may be fewer of these pockets, but when you find them, your probability of finding fish increases dramatically.

Dirty water places a premium on your ability to read the river and the behavior of its currents. Keying on those changes—structure, depth, current seams, and so forth—is far more important on dirty-water days than it is when you can spot fish through clear water. On dirty days, you have to use your brain and not just your eyes alone. A lot of people enjoy that. —**K.D.**

PART FOUR

Bugs: 43 Tips to Help You Select, Rig, and Fish the Right Fly at the Right Time in the Right Way

One of our goals in writing this book is to help you figure out what to tie onto the end of your tippet on a given day, and then catch a fish. Trout mostly eat insects and small fish. For you to catch them, your offerings generally have to resemble the real things.

To zero in on the right fly pattern for the right situation, you need a basic understanding of the different insects and their stages.

The insects trout eat are divided into different classes: mayflies (the oldest winged insects in existence, dating back roughly 370 million years; the wings of an adult look like a

sail on a boat); stoneflies (big, meaty staples in many rivers); midges (usually tiny); caddis (moth-like flies that inhabit many rivers nationwide); and terrestrials (land walkers, as the name implies, like grasshoppers and ants).

To figure out what fly to fish with, follow these three steps. Step one is to decide which classes or classes of insect are the trout most likely keyed on? Late summer, clear day, probably a terrestrial. Spring day, cloudy, a good bet for mayflies or caddis. Early June, high water, you'll know where the stoneflies are hatching. Midges are year-round bugs, but staples in winter, especially in tailwater rivers below dams.

Step two is to divide class by species. Which mayfly species, for example, is hatching now? This all depends on where you are, and the water and weather conditions. There are generalities you can follow. *Baetis*, for example, typically hatch in spring and fall. Hendricksons and Quill Gordons are classic spring bugs in the East (hence the name, mayflies). Gray Drakes and *Hexagenia* are June bugs in Michigan. Green Drakes are July–August (rainy day) insects in Colorado, and so forth.

Caddis love springtime (hence the Mother's Day caddis hatch), and the big stonefly hatches (like those on Rock Creek and the Big Hole in Montana) happen in June.

Any simple hatch chart will give you a general idea of what hatches where and when, and for the most part all they are good for are generalized guidelines.

Step three is division by insect stage. Insects live their life in stages. Once an insect hatches from its egg, it lives as a nymph in the river. The nymphal stage is the caterpillar to the butterfly, for all intents and purposes. The vast, vast majority of an insect's total lifespan is spent as a nymph. There are always nymphs in the river, every season, in all conditions. Moreover, when fish are feeding on dry flies, you can and should always assume they are eating nymphs as well.

The emerger is the insect transitioning from nymphal form to adulthood, ascending to the river surface to sprout its wings and fly away.

The dun is the recently emerged adult, drying its wings on the surface before it can fly away. This is the most vulnerable insect stage. Trout love it. Anglers love it. Fishing the dun is classic dry fly fishing.

The adults will fly around, mate, and do nothing else, as they don't have mouths and are unable to eat. This takes only a day or two. The adults mate, the females lay their eggs, they die, and the whole cycle starts over.

Take three steps—pinpoint the type of insect, species of insect, and stage of insect—and you take the mystery and guesswork out of bug selection. —**K.D.**

143. Dance Partners

It's become standard practice for many anglers to fish two flies at the same time. Double your flies and you double your odds, right?

Not always.

It's important to match your fly pairs with solid rationale. For example, one of the more common approaches is to fish dry-dropper, meaning you're fishing a dry fly on the surface and a nymph or emerger suspended about 18 inches below. You want the dry to be buoyant enough to float with the added weight of the fly below, and, likewise, you want the nymph to sink quickly.

But let's take that a step further. Maybe you want your dry fly to imitate the adult form of the insect, and the nymph to imitate the immature form of the same bug.

Or, perhaps you want your top fly to be an attractor, while the real meal is the morsel below. Or maybe you want that top fly to serve as nothing more than an indicator so you can keep your eyes trained on the strike zone.

It's all fair game, but think things through when you're matching one fly with another. —**K.D.**

144. Fishing Dirty

Dirty water should prompt you to do two things with your fly selection: go bigger and go brighter. A little extra flash and a little more profile are usually all you need to turn the fish on. —**K.D.**

145. Streamers

The key to streamer fishing is to throw your conventional dry fly and nymph thinking out the window. When fishing dries and nymphs, you want to minimize drag and motion. With streamer fishing, you want to max that out.

Tim Romano is one of the best streamer fishers we know, and he makes a point of choosing fly patterns that oscillate and exaggerate motion under the water—just as a panicked baitfish would.

Color selection is also a key consideration for Tim. As a rule, he chooses darker flies for darker, dirtier water, and lighter flies for clearer water. Olives and browns are his go-to colors in more neutral situations.

When retrieving streamers, Tim mixes up the length and speed of his strips in order to find a tempo that the trout prefer. Once he finds the correct tempo—and it can change from day to day—he sticks with it. Another rule of thumb is to slow the retrieve in colder and dirtier currents, and speed it up in clear water, especially when water temperatures are in the 55- to 65-degree range that trout prefer. —**K.D.**

146. Muddling Along

Given the difficult choice of choosing one fly to fish a trout river on a given day when there is no obvious hatch happening, I'd pick the Muddler Minnow. Why? Because the Muddler has multiple personalities, and it can be fished in different ways to cover a variety of situations.

Its primary role is that of streamer. Pulled below the surface, it looks like a sculpin or another baitfish. If you grease the deer hair on a Muddler, however, and either dead drift it on the surface or twitch it slightly under a cut bank, it looks very much like a grasshopper.

All flies can assume different characteristics if the angler understands how to adapt their presentations. Clip the wings and hackles on an Adam's dry fly, for example, and you've just made an impromptu RS2 emerger. Dead drift that black Woolly Bugger, and it becomes a leech (a favorite trout meal) carried downstream in the current.

The point is, don't be afraid to push the limits and adapt your flies to different situations. You don't always need 50 different patterns to match 50 scenarios. You are better off to carry ten flies and know how to fish each effectively, five different ways. —**K.D.**

147. Use an Attractor Fly

One of the best lessons I learned from scuba diving with trout came from watching them react to attractor flies. To set the scene, I had a buddy fishing a two-fly dry-fly rig. The lead fly was a size 12 Stimulator—a big ugly bug that might look like a terrestrial or a stonefly, although its basic mission is, as the name implies, to stimulate a rise. The second fly, trailed 18 inches off the hook shank of the first, was a size 18 Blue-Winged Olive, meant to match the natural *baetis* flies that pop up on the surface now and again.

As I watched the fish from below the surface, time and time I noticed them swim up to check out the larger fly, then catch view of the smaller fly and go eat it. The lesson is that if you are fishing two small dry flies, you won't draw their attention as consistently as you would by using an attractor dry fly.

The same applies to nymph fishing, particularly in swift currents or in tinted water. Your first should be a big ugly bug—maybe a hot pink San Juan Worm or a size 14 Flashback Pheasant Tail. Your trailer fly should be something smaller, perhaps a size 18 Barr Emerger. The fish are going to turn on the big bug that attracts their attention. Sometimes they'll eat it, but usually they'll pass on it in favor of the smaller fly. And they won't eat the smaller fly as consistently if you don't have an attractor bug drawing them in in the first place.

The attractor fly really only works when you are prospecting and when there isn't a consistent hatch coming off. When you're fishing a prolific hatch, don't mess around with attractors. —**K.D.**

148. Use a Spotter Fly

You can use a larger fly so you can spot a rise and take when the fly you are *really* fishing is too small or dark to see at a distance. One example occurred when I was fishing the basin below the bridge over Silver Creek in Idaho. The trout were eating beetles, so I tied on a size 14 black foam pattern, which came pretty close to imitating the real things.

The problem was that the wind made washboard waves on the surface; past 20 feet and I couldn't see the fly. To counter that, I tied on a size 10 Turck's Tarantula, then trailed the beetle below it.

With any disturbance or splash near the big, visible fly, I'd set the hook, and find that the trout had eaten the beetle. As a bonus, about every fifth fish or so ate the Tarantula.

In effect, you use the spotter fly as a strike indicator. Only it's better than a yarn or foam indicator, because it looks like a bug and is less likely to spook fish; plus, you might catch some fish in the process.

I will always use a fly as a strike indicator over foam or yarn when I can get away with it, and that's pretty much every situation except classic deep-run high-stick nymphing. —**K.D.**

149. **Below-the-Surface Spotter**

In really clear water, like that of the Frying Pan River in Colorado, guide Kea Hause shuns the classic nymph-rig strike indicator and instead uses a bright spotter fly such as a white San Juan Worm. He can see the white fly as it drifts through the run, just below the surface. Any subtle deviation in its course, any slight stagger or stop, and he assumes a fish just took the small Black Beauty nymph that's trailing behind the San Juan Worm.

Looks natural, doesn't spook fish, and it's connected right to the bug you're really fishing. —**K.D.**

150. **Make It a Meal**

The midge hatch is on. I'm fishing with guide Dan Stein, and swarms of tiny insects are littering the river's surface. Every trout in the Bighorn seems to be eating dry flies.

I reach into my fly box and poke around for a size 24 black midge pattern.

"That's no good," Dan said. "You won't see it and the fish won't eat it."

Instead of that tiny fly, Dan dipped into his fly box for a size 14 Blue Dun, a fly that looked absolutely nothing like the naturals on the water.

I wondered what in the world he was thinking, and he knew it.

"Just watch," he said. "Throw that fly upstream from the fish you just saw rising by the bank, and let it drift down."

I made the cast, and within a split second natural midges started landing on my fly. By the time it floated into the fish's feeding zone, it was a meatball of swarming insects. Sure enough, the brown trout rose to inhale the meatball fly, and I set the hook.

"You have to make it a meal," Dan said, smiling. "Why would a fish waste time and energy to suck down one little bitty bug? When the midges are hatching thick, always fish a midge cluster, or use a fly the bugs can cluster on. The more protein a fish sees, the more likely it is to eat." —**K.D.**

151. The Color Purple

The hot patterns in my fly box aren't new patterns, but rather purple variations of the old ones: purple Prince nymphs, purple San Juan Worms, purple Woolly Buggers, even purple Parachute Adamses.

No matter how hard you look, you won't find an insect that looks even remotely like a purple Prince nymph. But I know many guides use it when the chips are down. Other anglers gravitate to purple in tough conditions as well, from offshore

captains trolling purple skirts for tuna, to salmon guides in Alaska who prefer blue or purple beads, to bass pros who like purple-shaded soft plastics.

One theory is that purple catches fishes' eyes better than other shades. Among trout, for example, we know, according to Dr. Robert Behnke, author of *Trout and Salmon in North America*, that the cones in the retinas of trout eyes are more receptive to shades on the blue side of the spectrum. Behnke cautions, however, that trout "exhibit different feeding patterns at different times; during some periods, imitation of the food item of the moment is required." In other words, when they're on a hatch, matching size and color is key, but when they are just opportunity feeding, gaudy is better.

Recognize when fish are on a specific bite or not. When they are, match it, but when they are not—when you're just trying to get their attention—consider going purple. —**K.D.**

152. **Prince Nymph Mystery**

There is a difference between flies that look like something a trout is willing to eat and flies that look exactly like natural insects in a river. They are often one in the same, but not always.

Take the curious case of the Prince nymph. Montana guide Rusty Vorous once put the uncanny magnetism of the Prince nymph in perspective when he said: "You can walk up and down the whole river, turn over 1,000 rocks, and never find a bug that looks exactly like a Prince nymph."

So what is it about the Prince that makes it work? Some say the peacock-herl body looks just buggy enough to tempt any fish. Others claim its profile is an ideal generic shape to match a wide range of insects. Others like the way it moves in the water.

I have no idea why it works so well. I just know it does, and for my money, when I am nymph fishing—especially when I am fishing a tandem rig on a freestone river—the Prince is almost always my leader fly. —**K.D.**

153. **Bad Beadheads**

Beadhead flies are all the rage, and with good reason. Not only does that bead replicate the air bubble often found around a swimming or emerging bug, but the weight of the bead sinks the fly right into the strike zone. For fishing a dry-dropper rig, the beadhead is a natural dropper choice. In heavy currents, it's money.

Don't get hung up on fishing bead-headed flies in all situations, however. In slow-moving currents, and especially on flat ponds and lakes, the bead may do you more harm than good because it can sink too quickly and then get hung up on the bottom.

Use this simple gauge: If the current is moving slower than one foot per second, forget about the beads. —**K.D.**

154. **The Story Behind the Copper John**

John Barr is one of the most celebrated fly tiers in the world. His Copper John pattern is one of the hottest-selling flies for one good reason: It catches a lot of fish. To that point, I once fished a remote river in Chile with guide Ricardo Ellena. We spotted a fish that wasn't very interested in dry flies, so we decided to try nymphs. What pattern? I pulled a red size 16 Copper John from my box and offered it up for my guide's approval.

"Ah, *sí*," he said. "That is *la mosca assasina* (the killer fly), *el cobre de Juan* (the copper of John)."

I later told that story to John Barr and he laughed. Then he told me how that bug came to be.

Seems he was fishing years ago in the late summer, using a hopper-dropper rig. His bottom fly (a Barr Emerger) wasn't quite getting down to the fish as quickly and efficiently as he wanted it to.

So J. B. went back to his tying bench and whipped up a pattern that was sure to sink. He made the body out of copper wire, he put a bead head on it, then he added a few buggy accents such as a wing case and tail. By his own admission, this fly was meant to be an anchor that looked like an insect . . . sort of.

The funny thing is, once he fished that fly, the trout went absolutely nuts over it. Within a few years, it became Umpqua's hottest-selling fly pattern worldwide. Thousands of dozens are sold every year, in various of shades and sizes.

In other words, the hottest fly pattern in the world came to be almost by default, to make other flies work better.

The moral of the story is that weight is always a critical factor in fly selection. Having a fly that gets in the zone is as important, if not more important, than having a fly that looks natural. Having a fly with appeal, and function, is supernatural.
—**K.D.**

155. Size Matters

Of everything you have to consider when selecting a fly, size is the most important, especially during a hatch when trout are keyed to a particular insect. If you think you've identified whatever bug the trout are eating and they're refusing it, try going at

least one hook size smaller.

The same strategy holds for nymphing. If you know a river holds a certain insect, yet the fish are refusing your imitation, try a smaller version of the one you first tied on. Everyone loves those times and places during nonspecific feeding conditions when trout go for larger flies above and below the surface. With increased angling pressure almost everywhere, however, such situations can be difficult to find.

Heavily pressured trout sense danger in big flies. When in doubt, think small. —C.M.

156. **Reading the Rise**

The disturbance a trout makes when it takes a fly on the surface reveals much about what, and how, it is eating. A slow, deliberate rise generally means the prey is a mayfly resting on or near the surface. A splashy move for unseen insects typically is indicative of a midge. Fluttering caddis also elicit splashy rises, but these insects can generally be seen and identified in the air. And there's no mistaking the signs of a stonefly hatch. These large insects look like battleships on the surface; trout slurp them with gusto.

As a corollary, certain movements tell the specifics of the insect, particularly with mayflies. A normal rise means the trout is taking an insect on the surface. A porpoising rise, in which the fish sequentially shows its head and tail, generally indicates an insect in the surface film. A bulge, with only a back showing, points to a fish feeding on emergers that haven't quite reached the top. —C.M.

157. **Pumping for Information**

Even experienced anglers sometimes have trouble figuring out what trout are eating when several different insects are on the surface. For example, you may observe fish rising amid a huge mayfly hatch, but can't get a hit on what seems a realistic imitation.

The dilemma may be the result of a shadow hatch of a smaller insect that, for some odd reason, has become the center of the fish's attention. In such cases, a suction stomach pump, available in most trout shops, can be invaluable. Use it carefully, so you don't injure the fish, and you'll quickly discover what's on the menu. —**C.M.**

158. Dishing Up the Facts

Suppose you can't catch that first fish to perform a stomach scrutiny? Many anglers carry a portable seine so they can take a quick surface census. Lefty Kreh, noted for his clever ideas, cites a handy alternative. Cut out the bottom from an ordinary soap dish and replace it with a fine-mesh wire. When you put it in the water, insects will collect in the mesh for easy identification. You can keep them available for later inspection by simply closing the lid. —**C.M.**

159. Quick-Change Artist

In this same vein, one of the most vital elements of success rests with the ability to switch flies, or even make a complete

adjustment in tactics, when conditions turn. On streams, conditions rarely stay the same for long. Hatches come and go; trout move from one insect to another; focus changes from top to bottom.

Those moments when fish are feeding aggressively are precious. Stay alert, and be ready to make a quick transformation right along with trout. —**C.M.**

160. Time Is Fish

Tournament fishermen know the supreme value of time. Bass pros keep several rods loaded with a wide variety of lures, switching from one to the next until they find what's working. They make every minute count. These options generally aren't available to fly fishermen, but there are ways to reduce annoying down time, such as tangles with multiple fly rigs that steal long minutes, and, in the case of float fishing, hundreds of yards of precious water.

The solution? Prepare several such rigs in advance. When you get a snarl, quickly snip off the offending tippet and tie on another—a quick, one-knot process. The extras can be wrapped neatly on a piece of cardboard inside a plastic zipper bag. You'll catch more fish and, as important, avoid a lot of mental anguish. —**C.M.**

161. The Corset Connection

God never made an insect with rubber legs. Fly tyers, of course, do, and trout just eat them up. The reason is that most fish are titillated by anything bite-size that exudes life. Years ago, someone made a fly wiggly and jiggly by using rubber fibers from those elastic devices used to shape women's figures. Thus, the Girdle Bug was born.

Imaginative tyers have since contrived to attach rubber legs to all sorts of patterns, almost always with satisfactory results. There's a general message here about attracting fish, particularly with larger flies. You'll seldom go wrong if you make a fly look alive. Like a housecat teased with a piece of yarn, trout can't resist the tantalizing action of rubber legs presented with just the right twitch. The visibility of white rubber also makes this a particularly effective pattern in murky water. —**C.M.**

162. The Early Fly Gets Eaten

Crowding is a reality when fishing desirable public water these days, which makes arriving early—a good strategy under almost any circumstance—an even better idea. With a brain the size of a pea, a trout isn't the brightest creature on the planet. But trout do have the ability to learn from constant intrusions into their environment. After being exposed to parades of anglers, assorted flies, and occasional stings in the mouth from those flies, fish become far less likely to bite.

There's a real advantage in getting to the water ahead of the crowds. You'll also find a stealth benefit from low-light conditions in the early morning. Trout are also more likely to look up for a fly without a bright late-morning sun beaming into their eyes. —**C.M.**

163. Through the Looking Glass

Most fishermen know the value of polarized glasses in penetrating surface glare to spot fish. To use those glasses most efficiently, it helps to develop an understanding of where trout are likely to be. That way, you'll spend less time staring into blank water.

Less understood is the benefit to be gained from binoculars in seeing subtle rise rings and other movements from distant vantage points, such as high embankments. Not only can a compact set of binoculars be a valuable fishing aid, it can also help you better enjoy viewing wildlife along the stream. —**C.M.**

164. Lightening the Load

Considering the current proliferation of flies, it isn't all that far-fetched to suggest that a well-supplied angler might need to rent a forklift to transport all his boxes to the water. Never have there been so many fine flies to entice both fish and fishermen. Anyone with a bit of imagination and a fat wallet can load up in a hurry.

Which basic patterns do we choose? The traditional Adams represents most dark-colored mayflies. A Pale Morning Dun pattern takes care of the lighter ones. Elkhair caddis in various sizes and shades cover the water for that species. Beneath the surface, a Gold-ribbed Hare's Ear nymph represents a variety of insects. Add a Pheasant Tail to mimic mayflies, a caddis larva, caddis emerger, and various sizes of stoneflies, and you've got what you need for most situations. An assortment of attractor patterns should handle the rest. —**C.M.**

165. Behind the Mask

One of the most challenging situations in fly fishing occurs when multiple hatches are in progress on the same piece of water. The dreaded masking hatch occurs when it appears that trout are rising greedily to a certain insect—usually the most visible of the lot—when they're actually eating something else.

An experienced angler first examines the rise form, which typically will be splashy for caddisflies or midges and more subtle for mayflies. With time and observation, an angler learns to detect which stage of an emerging insect is drawing the most attention. —**C.M.**

166. Cure for the Muddy Water Blues

Many fly fishermen pack it in when rivers run high and off-color during runoff following a heavy rain. Instead, they'd be better served to view this as an opportunity. Trout don't stop eating when the water rises; far from it. High water often carries an abundance of food, including worms and insects dislodged by the flow.

Fish aren't picky about what they eat during such times. They also must make faster decisions in dirty water, and thus are easier to catch.

In muddy water, try a streamer, large stonefly, or something offbeat and splashy, such as a rubber-leg pattern. This could be the time to catch the biggest fish of the season. —**C.M.**

167. Reconnecting with an Old Friend

In our modern infatuation with all the various applications of nymphs, we've neglected a method that long formed the bedrock of fly fishing. The traditional wet fly, as it imitates the emerging form of many insects, remains one of the most effective techniques for attracting aggressive trout hunting in the middle depths.

Cast soft-hackle patterns quartering downstream with enough weight to sink them. Let the fly work through prime holding spots with a series of lifts that imitate an insect swimming or drifting toward the surface. At the end of the drift, let the fly hang briefly in the current.

Don't be afraid to try a double-fly rig with this method, perhaps using a soft-hackle wet behind a conventional nymph to imitate two different kinds of insects. —**C.M.**

168. Wake-up Call

You see insects on the water, but every dry fly you choose in an attempt to match the hatch is met with a refusal. First you're puzzled, then frustrated, then dejected.

Don't get mad—get even.

As the instrument of your revenge, try an attractor. This can be a large dry fly, a streamer, even a big nymph. The notion is to offer the trout an attention-getter that's impossible to ignore. Besides, the switch to larger flies generally makes things easier and more fun.

Not every trout will take the come-on, but the tactic will often attract enough trout to turn a slow day into success. Then you won't feel frustrated any more. —**C.M.**

169. The Living Fly

Wayne Maca, a bamboo rod designer from Montana, devised a large floating fly whose most visible feature is a closed-cell foam body for maximum flotation. There's nothing startling about this, as fly tyers have been using foam for years. Maca also adds rubber legs, which is nothing special either.

What Maca does next is the really creative part. He ties in, of all things, a marabou wing and tail, an odd combination for a surface fly. The result is a floater with tantalizing motion, one that moves like a living organism. It can be twitched and teased for exceptionally long drifts along a tight bank or extended current seams.

With a play on words, Maca calls his creation the "Serial Killer." Asked what it imitates, he doesn't hesitate to reply.

"Bait," he says. The lesson: Dry-fly dead drifts are good. Something that looks alive can be even better. —**C.M.**

170. The Invisible Caddis

More than any other important aquatic insect, caddisflies spend very little time on the surface. Common to virtually every river or lake, these insects emerge quickly, break the surface in a burst, and then are gone.

Most feeding activity during caddis hatches takes place on the emerging pupae. In their enthusiasm to capture the rapidly moving pupae, trout often make splashes on the surface or even leap into the air. This gives the appearances that fish are rising to dry flies when, in fact, no adult flies are on the water.

At this stage, it's far more important to imitate this upward movement of the pupae than to dabble in the adult flies that can be seen flying about, but are seldom involved in the feeding sequence. Trout that follow emerging caddis to the surface can be tempted by skittering a high-floating dry fly—a pattern made or deer or elk hair—across the surface, but the subsurface tactic is going to catch you more fish in the long run. —**C.M.**

171. Cold-Water Cure: Brighten Up

Fish are cold-blooded, with a metabolism that's tightly linked to temperature. This means that they don't eat as much or react as quickly when the water is extremely cold. Successful anglers stand ready to offer a little help.

One way to do this is to slow down the drift, using extra weight or line manipulation to make the fly move slightly slower than the current.

Another is to choose a more visible fly that the trout can see coming a little sooner. Apart from helping a fly sink, this is one of the primary benefits of beadheads. Flies that incorporate bright metal or glass beads work well all year, but are particularly effective during winter. —**C.M.**

172. Damsels in Distress

Perhaps this has happened to you. You're fishing a quiet lake or pond, and you've pushed out near the tops of your waders to make that hero cast to where you think the trout are. At some point in this process, you become aware that trout are swirling behind you, between you and the shore.

Chances are, you've waded smack into the middle of an emergence of damselflies, among the most common and perhaps least utilized of the aquatic insect species. We all know about these fairy-winged insects that flit around the margins of still water. But few anglers realize the importance they play in the diet of trout and the sensational action they can provide.

We occasionally see trout leaping for the fluttering adults. Indeed, an imitation of a winged damsel sometimes prompts explosive strikes from trout keyed to the surface. But it's the subsurface migration of the emergers that holds the key to more enduring success.

A bit of entomology is in order. A member of the same order as dragonflies, damsels spend most of their lives as developing nymphs amid aquatic vegetation in still or slow-moving water. When a biologic signal arrives, usually in May and early June, they begin a swift and deliberate migration toward shore. Using flagella in their tails, which also contain the gills, they wiggle rapidly toward the closest object connected to the surface, shed their exoskeleton, and emerge in the flight form.

It's the jaunt to shore that's so important to anglers. Trout congregate in the shallows to intercept these two-inch-long insects, often becoming absolute fools for imitations stripped briskly to imitate the erratic path of the natural. Damsel emergers come in two basic colors: olive and brown. Make sure you always have some in your fly box. —C.M.

173. Seeing Double

Despite the increased likelihood of tangles and snarls, double- or even triple-nymph rigs are gaining popularity. Why? Because you've just doubled or tripled the chances that you have some-thing tied to your line a fish might try to eat.

The standard reasoning is to use a large attractor fly, usually weighted, closest to the fly line. Allow for at least a nine-inch spacing to your trailer fly, a smaller nymph that imitates the prevailing insect. A split shot or two above the lead fly completes the rig. Typically, a fish moves on the attractor and, if that proves unsatisfactory, switches to the trailer.

Don't despair about casting this catastrophe-in-waiting. It can be done. Avoid trying to fling it for distance. The key is to accelerate the delivery so the leader and all its accoutrements completely turn over and land in a straight line on the water. —C.M.

174. Color Coding

How fish see colors is primarily affected by the amount of light entering the water; the less light, the less visible some colors become. The shortest waves, blue and green, are absorbed slowly, while reds are absorbed quickly. As a rule, choose blue and green for deep-water baitfish patterns or in areas where the water is murky. Also consider that red is the most visible and, in some cases, most vital color for aggressive predators feeding in shallow water. Many say that the red closely imitates the flared gills of an alarmed baitfish, which can trigger a fast response from feeding trout. —C.M.

175. Get the Red In

Some years ago, noted author and angler Robert H. Boyle conducted an experiment in which he repeatedly introduced minnows into a sizeable aquarium containing largemouth bass. Half were ordinary silver shiners; the other half were shiners that had been dyed red. Through repeated tests, the bass demonstrated a profound preference for the crimson minnows. We know of no similar test for salmonids, but it helps explain why so many successful fly patterns contain a splash of red. —**C.M.**

176. **Sharpie Thinking**

Along the lines of adapting flies on the move and in the river, guide John Flick of Durango, Colorado, often carries a black Sharpie permanent marker in his pocket. When he finds that tan caddis are over-matched by black caddis on the river, for example, a few strokes of the pen changes the fly's color, and puts him right in the game. A few dabs on a PMD can also make that mayfly pattern something completely different. —**K.D.**

177. **Love Ants and Beetles**

The most overlooked and under-loved dry flies in the world are ants and beetle patterns. I don't know why this is, as you'll find ants and beetles on almost any decent trout river in the world, and trout love eating them.

If you're worried about not being able to see a small black beetle or ant on the water, use a pattern with a red, white, or orange post or patch on its back to make it more visible. Failing that, use an attractor fly with your ant or beetle: See the hopper, fish the ant.

Don't neglect to fish ants and beetles, especially when there is no major hatch going on and you see fish suspended in shallow water near the bank or next to structures such as logs and cut banks. Those fish are opportunistic feeders, and odds are they'll hit a well-placed ant or beetle. —**K.D.**

178. Going Goo-Goo

Be careful not to put too much flotant gel on a fly before you cast it. Use just enough grease to make its color darker, as if you dunked it in the water. Big silicone globs sticking to a fly's hackles are enough to turn off any trout.

Grease flies when they come out of the box and before the first cast. After awhile, as the flotant wears off, use a dry-shake powder to dry them off and get them riding high again. Never grease flies that are already wet. —**K.D.**

179. Barbless

To fish barbless or not? That is the question. Here is my answer: Assuming the angler knows how to maintain good fighting pressure on a trout, I have never seen a situation where the lack of a barb on a fly has been the determining factor in landing the fish or not.

On another note, I have seen several situations where a flattened barb on a streamer stuck in the face of a guide has been the determining factor in requiring an impromptu minor surgery, or merely calling it an inconvenient hiccup in the day.

It's a no-brainer.

Always fish barbless. Doing so is good for trout, even better for people. —**K.D.**

180. Are You a Good Twitch, or a Bad Twitch?

Sometimes a little twitch of a dry fly can be a good thing, an attention getter. This is especially true when you're fishing flies that imitate bugs that skitter naturally, such as caddis, stoneflies, and grasshoppers.

If you spot a fish, make a cast, and come up a little out of range; make a short, subtle twitch or two before picking up and casting again. It may be just what you need to prod a trout into action.

The twitch factor is why many flies—especially terrestrials—that incorporate wiggly rubber legs are so effective. —**K.D.**

181. Flatwater Flies

In the West, the predominant mid- to late-summer mayfly of choice on flat waters such as spring creeks and lakes is *callibaetis*. For adult *callibaetis*, if you want to catch gulpers, it's hard to beat a CDC wing *callibaetis* pattern, or a no-hackle, with a simple duck feather wing, pale body, and extended tail.

Don't overlook the option of slowly twitching and swimming nymphs near shoreline vegetation. For that game, Shane Stalcup's Gilled Nymph is the money bug. —**K.D.**

182. Up on Cripple Creek

Fishing the "S" curves section of Idaho's Silver Creek with guide Dave Faltings, I encountered some of the most finicky trout I've ever seen. They were rising. In fact, we could see their mouths as they sipped from the surface. We tried at least four or five different *callibaetis* dry-fly patterns, and were consistently refused.

Dave decided we should try a crippled mayfly pattern, which imitates an emerger that can't get out of its shuck. The insect has reached the surface, but is stuck there, paralyzed, and completely at the mercy of the trout. The fly we used had a post and hackle wrapped at an angle, so the tip and head rode above the surface, and the body dangled in the film.

First cast, a big trout ate the fly.

In the years since, I have consistently found that in any hatch situation, when trout are keyed on a specific insect, be it Green Drakes, *callibaetis*, Hendricksons, or Blue Quills, but you're getting refused or ignored altogether, it's worth fishing a cripple. The cripple is your last, best shot, and it often works. —**K.D.**

183. Ten Flies to Never Leave Home Without

The Woolly Bugger. This is a go-to trout-producing streamer that can be fished effectively on lakes and rivers.

The Pheasant Tail Nymph: A generic pattern, it represents a wide range of immature mayflies.

The Prince Nymph: This is probably the best all-around attractor nymph pattern you can use.

The Parachute Adams: A generic-looking adult mayfly, when wet its gray body can effectively match many insect species.

The Pale Morning Dun: A midsummer staple on many rivers, east and west, this is the mayfly pattern that matches insects with pale bodies (yellow, pink, cream).

The Copper John: Another attractor nymph, it's valued as much for its weight and sink-ability as for its flashy profile.

The Elk Hair Caddis: Use this dry fly on any rivers where caddis hatch in large numbers.

Black Foam Beetle: It won't sink, and it's a killer pattern for fish keyed on terrestrials, anywhere.

The Barr Emerger: Pale Morning Dunn or Blue-winged Olive varieties fool the most selective trout.

The Muddler Minnow: It's a streamer and grasshopper, all in one. —**K.D.**

184. The Next 10 Best

Kaufmann's Stimulator: This is a great attractor dry fly that can represent anything from terrestrials to stoneflies and Green Drakes.

The San Juan Worm: The T-bone steak of the trout world, some anglers consider it dirty pool.

The Glo-Bug: Never underestimate a trout's affinity for eggs (see dirty pool).

The Chernobyl Ant: This is a deadly, high-riding terrestrial; fish it under trees, near cut banks.

The Zebra Midge: With a tungsten beadhead, this simple little pattern is a midge staple.

Graphic Caddis: When you fishing caddis waters, you'll find this to be an almost unbeatable nymph pattern.

Stonefly Nymph: In yellow and/or brown, it imitates the protein mother-lode trout crave.

The Rusty Spinner: Easy pickings for trout, this represents the spent adult mayfly.

Tricos: It's important to match this hatch accurately when trout are dialed in.

Humpy: Use it when you need extra buoyancy in faster water; mix and match the colors. —**K.D.**

185. Mousing Around

By day, trout are wary, reclusive fish that fin in deep currents and sip insects discriminately. At night, however, you'll encounter a Dr. Jekyll–Mr. Hyde contrast in trout behavior—especially big trout behavior—if you fish a mouse fly.

Swim a hairy critter across the deep pool by the logjam where *you just know* Mr. Brown Trout must to be hanging out. Cast against the bank, start stripping the fly with short erratic strips and pauses, and wait for the crash.

You know those pictures you see in the fly-shop brochures, where the guy is holding a gigantic trout taken from waters that you fish often, but have yet to catch anything over 18 inches long? Odds are that angler was fishing with a mouse fly. —**K.D.**

PART FIVE

Miscellaneous: 65 Tips on Fighting Fish, Wading, Choosing Gear, and Everything Else That Matters

186. Firmer Footing

There's no stepping around it: At times our angling success will depend upon how well we wade. Whether it's a brawling British Columbia steelhead river or a slippery brook, the ability to reach the right position may be the most important factor in catching that special fish.

In a similar vein, the ability to wade with confidence has much to do with our overall enjoyment of the experience on-stream, whether we catch anything or not.

The fact is, it's practically impossible to enjoy fishing if every step along a rocky streambed leaves us afraid of a dunking. Fear shouldn't be a part of the angling experience.

Good equipment is the first step to safe wading. It begins with a solid sole for gripping rocks. Either rubber or felt soles work fine, though you must thoroughly clean felt after each day of fishing, so you don't carry invasive species to other waters. If the stones of your favorite streams also come with a slick coating of algae, as is often the case with nitrogen-enriched tailwaters or other altered environments, buy boots with studs that can bite through slime into the rock.

Once you've acquired the proper gear, including a stout wading staff, relax, bend your knees, and enjoy. —**C.M.**

187. **Rocks Don't Swim**

I recently enjoyed a spring day of fishing with my friend Dennis Swift. We had typical Colorado conditions: high water fueled by snowpack runoff, with fish feeding nymphs. To get our offerings down to the fish, we used tons of split shot to weight our rigs. Sure enough, Dennis snagged a rock, or so he thought. Frustrated, he started twitching and flicking his rod in different directions, trying to free himself; the line started to move upstream.

"Hang on, Dennis, that's a fish!" I yelled.

"Naw, it's a rock."

"No it's a fish!"

"How do you know?" he asked.

I instinctively answered, "Rocks don't swim!"

The point isn't to pick on poor Dennis, whose flies did come loose, after a giant rainbow that had begun the battle with uncommon lethargy suddenly cartwheeled across the river. Rather, it's to suggest that it's smart to treat every stop as a fish strike. Take your time. Set the hook gently, with little more energy than a military salute, and then wait a moment. If and when you know you're really, truly stuck, then give the rod some quick, tight tugs upstream. Jerking the rod in different directions will only dig you in deeper. —**K.D.**

188. **Walk Away from Trouble**

With the growing popularity of fly fishing, it's increasingly difficult to find the open space we all crave. The best way to beat angling pressure is to use your feet. Choose more difficult places or simply walk farther than the crowds do.

One secret to making this happen is to abstain from stringing your line until you reach your distant destination. This will help you resist the temptation to stop at attractive, yet heavily fished spots along the way.

The payoff comes in solitude and more fish on the line. —**C.M.**

189. **Boot Camp Basics**

If it's financially feasible, buy two different types of wading boots. One should have rubber soles with grids designed both to grip rocks yet allow for easy walking—particularly when the destination is some distant small stream where the wading isn't difficult. These same soles can be worn in drift boats or other places where cleats can cause damage.

The second pair should have rubber soles with metal studs, which are excellent for gripping rocks, especially those covered in algae. These more expensive boots tend to wear out quickly, especially if you're doing long hikes over rough terrain, which is why having a pair of rubber-soled boots makes sense. —**C.M.**

190. **Strip for Action**

We've all seen this guy: He's wearing the biggest vest he can buy, and all of the pockets are bulging with fly boxes, lines, leaders, flashlights, bug dope, and every other imaginable sort of paraphernalia. When he wades into the stream, his boots sink an extra six inches into the mud.

Chances are he'll only use about one-tenth of what he's carrying. What he'll end up using is also predictable. With a little forethought, our overstuffed angler could have left most of his gear in the vehicle.

Try streamlining your gear. Carry an effective assortment of flies for the day and leave the rest. The same applies to all the other special-situation gear that doesn't fit the day. Double this requirement if the outing involves a lot of walking. Over time, you'll refine your selection . . . and you'll rarely leave something you really need. —**C.M.**

191. Meshing with Your Cast

Lefty Kreh adopted this simple, yet effective way to avoid tangling his line on all the various appendages he finds in a boat: ropes, life jackets, anchors, knobs, and cracks. The old castmaster brings along an appropriately sized square of light mesh netting, which he spreads over the area where he'll coil his line. Presto, no more tangles. The mesh stuffs easily into a pocket or small pouch. —**C.M.**

192. Keeping Things Clean

You'll be surprised how quickly your fly line collects dirt and grime, a condition that can radically slow its progress through the guides, stealing valuable feet from your cast. The propensity for this is worse in boats, in salt water, or in water carrying a load of silt or muck.

Clean your line regularly using a strip of soft cloth and any of several commercial products with silicone in the mix. This treatment removes dirt while leaving a slick coating that shoots smoothly through the guides. The line will float higher and lift more easily from the water.

Regular cleaning also extends the life of the line. —**C.M.**

193. Cleared for Takeoff

In a time when air travel rules keep changing due to terrorism concerns, it's important to know what you can and can't take as carry-on. Frequent fliers are aware of the perils of lost luggage, and prefer to keep essentials such as flies, reels, and extra lines in their carry-on luggage. Since everyone packs extras, it's generally easier to borrow a rod for a couple days.

You never know what to expect at the security check, where regulations often vary from place to place. You hear horror stories about confiscation of fly lines or anything that might have a hook attached. To avoid trouble, make a point of asking your airline ahead of time about regulations at each place you plan to visit. —**C.M.**

194. It Isn't Psychoanalysis, But . . .

As far as we know, nobody has ever gotten into the head of a trout. Lee Wulff probably came as close as anyone. Renowned for his ability to catch large fish on tiny flies and light lines, Wulff had a distinct strategy for playing fish.

The theory, as the master angler expressed it, is that if you can break a horse or train a dog, you can pretty much do the same with a fish. Wulff believed that if you can confuse the trout you have on the line, you can dramatically lessen the time it takes to land him. This tactic involves keeping it off balance, chiefly by pulling it sideways when it tries to turn in the opposite direction.

Every fish swims strongest when either moving straight ahead or boring downstream. By pulling back over the top, you're playing to its strength. It takes much longer to tire a fish this way, and that increases the chance of angler error or hook or line failure. Pulling to the side will let you upset a trout's balance—and maybe even its psyche—and let you net it much more quickly. —**C.M.**

195. Dear Diary

We've all heard the adage that 10 percent of anglers catch 90 percent of the fish. Make up your own percentages; your guess is as good as any.

While skill definitely affects your catch rate, really successful anglers keep diaries and make entries about every fishing trip they take. Weather, air temperature, water temperature, insect activity, fish hooked, fish lost, flies used (both successfully and unsuccessfully)—everything goes into that diary. As the months and years go by, certain patterns start to stand out. You eventually will be able to figure out that you shouldn't fish stream X in May, but if you go there in June, you'll stand a good chance of success—especially if you use flies that have worked there before.

You can record all this cyclical information in the fancy log-books sold in high-end fly shops, perhaps in leather with a bit of gold trim, or you can use a ringed binder or even a pocket memo pad. Whichever tool you use, record your experiences and all those tips you receive along the way that otherwise might be forgotten. Use as much detail as necessary. It'll make for fascinating reading—and fishing—in the future. —**C.M.**

196. **Playing for Keeps**

When playing a large fish on light line, a sporting angler attempts to land it as quickly as possible to avoid harming or even killing the fish from excessive lactic acid buildup. This can best be achieved by keeping the rod tip low to the water while maintaining a 90-degree angle between rod tip and line as a hedge against breaking off. That way, you can turn the trout from side to side, knocking it off balance and generally avoiding those stronger muscles with which a fish swims straight ahead. —**C.M.**

197. **Why Women are Born Better Anglers than Men**

Scenario A: A husband and wife show up for a guided fishing day, and neither of them has ever fly fished before. Scenario

B: An intermediate-level male fly fisherman shows up for a guide trip with his wife. He wants to clue her in on the whole experience, and wants a guide to show her the ropes.

Ask 1,000 guides from California to Maine what's going to happen in either scenario, and 950 of them will tell you the same thing: She's going to catch more fish than he is. No, it's not because the guide is a womanizer and eager to spend most of his time with her. It's because she isn't going to spend the day fighting the effects of testosterone: powering the rod, pushing casts, getting into brawls with fish, being ultra competitive. Women in general are more patient than men in these situations, and the results will prove it. —**K.D.**

198. The Golden Rule

Under no circumstances should a man ever try to teach his wife or girlfriend, and a woman her husband or boyfriend, the mechanics of golf and fly fishing. That's what pros and guides are for. You can take my word for it, or you can learn the hard way. —**K.D.**

199. Crossing to Safety

There are ways to wade a river safely, and ways to ensure that you will get wet. Dale Darling, former owner of the St. Vrain Angler fly shop, has a few pointers for keeping dry. First, no matter how good your wading boots feel, you want to walk next to rocks, not on top of them. You never want to find yourself in a situation where your legs are crossed, or you'll lose your balance. Keep the toes of your boots pointed slightly upstream

at all times to maintain balance. And when you're crossing the river in swift current, pick a destination point at a 45-degree angle downstream from where you start, and cross on an angle. If there's an obvious deep spot, avoid it by choosing a path of embarkation and debarkation from the river that starts at point A, upstream, and ends at point B, roughly 45 degrees downstream. As a rule, don't step into unfamiliar waters where you cannot clearly see your boots. Wear polarized sunglasses to help you see the bottom. And always cross the river downstream. When you fight the current by pressing upstream, you will inevitably lose the battle. —**K.D.**

200. Dock Talk

Before he won the 2006 Bassmaster Classic, Luke Clausen told me that he doesn't pay much attention to dock talk. Tips on secret places, special lures (or flies), and can't-miss tactics are usually loss leaders. Better to trust your instincts and develop your own tunnel vision for finding the best places to cast a line, or not.

Fly fishing is a people sport, and the best guides are usually open books with their information, because they know they can duplicate their efforts on any given day, with any given clients, in most situations. Beware of the guide who tells you he has a secret spot, or a special approach, because more often than not, it's not true. Learn to develop your own instincts and abilities, and whether you pair that with a contender guide, or just set out on your own, you're going to be light years ahead of the person grasping for insightful information from anyone who will give it. Make your own breaks, then share them, not vice versa. —**K.D.**

201. **Keep the Arc**

The trick to landing big trout on a river isn't all that complicated. Yes, you are going to run into situations where a fish makes a sudden unexpected charge, and it snaps you off. That

happens to everyone. But when I'm guiding a beginner, I tell them that all they need to be concerned with, after the hookup, is maintaining a steady arc in the fly rod, with the tip high. You need a strong, solid flex; nothing more, nothing less. If the fish wants to run, let him go, but keep the strong flex arc in the rod. If you let the rod go flat to the waterline, because the fish is pulling and bursting, odds are it will break your tippet. If a fish runs at you and you aren't able to maintain a consistent arc in the rod, there's a good chance the fish will spit the fly.

Don't worry about the fish. Worry about the arc. Adjust as necessary, giving line to the fish when it runs, gathering it when you can. Keep the tip high and the rod flexed in a consistent arc, and everything else will take care of itself. You'll land more trout. —**K.D.**

202. **Timesaver Rigging**

We've all had this happen. You're fishing a two- or three-fly rig, with split shot, perhaps on a float trip. The bite is red hot, and then the inevitable happens. You foul up a cast, the rig performs a bolo twist, and you're stuck with the mother of all bird's nests. You've got two choices: Claw your way through the tangle or build a new rig. Either way, you're going to watch a lot of time and water go by.

There is a third alternative, however. If you know which rig you'll be using before you go fishing, put together several extras before leaving home. Peg them to a piece of stiff cardboard, lash them down with a couple rubber bands, and you're set for a quick change with a single knot connection when trouble strikes. —**C.M.**

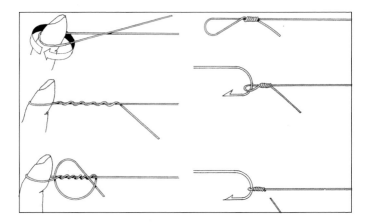

203. Clinch Knot on Your Finger

Every guide has a different rig strategy: space flies far apart or pack them tight; link flies with tippet eye-to-eye or make your connections off the hook-shank, and so on. There is no absolute right way to do any of this.

As far as hooking one fly to another is concerned, I will say this: When fishing a tandem fly rig, for the past 15 years I've done nothing but tie the trailer fly off the hook-shank of the lead fly: dry to dry, dry to dropper, nymph to nymph, it's all the same. Use an improved clinch knot on the lead fly, then tie the tippet to the hook-shank of that fly with another clinch knot, and then tie on a dropper.

That used to be an awkward exercise. I'd be standing there in the river, twisting the tippet around the hook of a fly, trying to make a knot from which I could secure a second fly, all the while trying to hold my fly rod under one arm.

I was doing this one day on the Snake River in Wyoming when guide Patty Reilly noticed my all-thumbs effort as I twisted monofilament around the shank of a hopper fly. "What on earth are you doing?" she asked.

When I explained, she made me stop, then showed me the single greatest knot-tying trick I've ever seen.

Want to connect one fly to another? Tie an improved clinch knot on your finger.

Take a strand of tippet, loop it over your index finger, then twist that index finger five or six times. Take the tag end of the tippet and thread it through the bottom V space in the line, then wrap it back through the top of the loop. Spit on the knot and pull it taut (but not so taut as to close the loop at the end of the tippet). You've just made a lariat-type knot that can wrap around any fly you want to connect to. —**K.D.**

204. **Those Dirty Dogs**

I was born a bait fisherman, and eventually gravitated toward spinfishing and baitcasting. Then I found fly fishing, and for a long while I was stuck right there, believing that all things on the fly were noble and good and that everything else was dirty pool. The more I have fly fished, however, the more I have come to respect those conventional fishing anglers, and look to them for guidance. In the end, while you might embrace fly fishing as your personal gold standard, it's never wise to look down your nose at anyone tossing the heavy metal. Before you judge, take time to study what they are doing and, if you are so inclined, transpose what you learn to your fly fishing. When you do it correctly, there are situations when fishing the fly on the long rod is the number-one deadliest approach to catching fish, bar none. But the best fly fishers are those who keep the blinders off, and are willing to learn a trick or two from the conventional tackle anglers. —**K.D.**

205. **Solving a Knotty Problem**

When fish are rising and precious yards of river are whizzing past your drift boat, any time lost tying a knot is pure agony. If the knot doesn't come quickly, it becomes torture. Learning to tie basic knots swiftly and securely may be the best gift any angler can give himself. Keep some monofilament handy and practice at home, while you're watching baseball on television. Don't worry if you miss a pitch or two. That's far better than losing valuable time on the water. —**C.M.**

206. **Stretching Out**

Few things in fly casting are more irritating, and debilitating, than stiff coils in the loose fly line you're trying to shoot through the guides. To help eliminate the coils that accumulate when a line is stored on the reel, stretch the line out when you're rigging up just before hitting the water. Simply loop the fly line around a smooth surface that won't snag the finish, such as a car door handle, and then back off the prescribed distance and pull tight. If you're with a fishing buddy, have him grab the end of the line and tug. —**C.M.**

207. Mark That Line

We've all made the mistake of removing a perfectly good line from a spool, then forgetting to mark its weight and design. The result is a drawer full of mystery lines that otherwise could be put to work. Lefty Kreh devised an ingenious coding system, using a waterproof marker and a series of dots and dashes, that lets him identify each line. You can also take a strip of masking tape and write down the proper identification on a storage or spare reel spool. Devise a system and use it, or else you're going to have a bunch of useless line on your hands. —**C.M.**

208. The Effects of Sunlight

With the possible exception of mosquito repellent and gasoline, sunlight—even in diffused form—is the ultimate enemy of monofilament, causing a radical weakening that can't be identified until you've broken off a nice fish. If you can't afford to replace several spools of expensive fluorocarbon each spring, make certain to store them in a case or drawer during the off-season. It also helps to zip loose spools into a vest pocket at the end of a fishing day or during transit in daylight hours. —**C.M.**

209. Velcro to the Rescue

On an outing that required a hike into a canyon, veteran Denver angler and world traveler Joy Hilliard revealed an innovation that solves several rod-line management problems. Rather than carry an unwieldy rod case that she'd eventually have to stash somewhere in the woods, she arranges her rod—already strung with fly and line—in two pieces. She uses a short piece of Velcro to tightly secure both ends of the rod. This allows the rod to be carried easily and safely. Upon reaching a river, all she has to do is remove the two Velcro strips, tuck them into a pocket, and she's ready to go fishing. —**C.M.**

210. Pick the Right Rod

If you want to get the ulti-mate satisfaction from a day on the water, it's critical to choose a rod that matches the situation. That won't happen if you need to deliver a weighty nymph rig and you're using a soft rod, or if you want to try delicate dry-fly presentations and you have a rod that's too stiff or heavy. Spend some time considering the likely demands of the day, make the proper rod choices, and you'll be off to a good start. —**C.M.**

211. Putty in Our Hands

Apart from environmental concerns, there's a strategically sound reason to use non-lead, pinch-on weight. You'll save on lost flies. When a soft weight snags on bottom, it will often come off the line. The result is a lost pinch of tungsten, not an expensive fly. —**C.M.**

212. Newspaper Knowledge

A wise old angler once made a point to me by using a medium-sized streamer hook and a rolled-up newspaper. Taking the hook, he stuck the barb into the paper as hard as he could. Despite the pressure, it barely penetrated a few pages and didn't come close to burying the barb. Clearly, the hook would have been no match for the bony jaw of the big fish. Many larger hooks or flies aren't sharp enough to do the job when new; make a point of sharpening them. —**C.M.**

213. Making That Point

As a follow-up to the previous passage, it pays to get the sharpening done before reaching the water. First, test the point on the back of your thumbnail to determine its sharpness. If you tie your own flies, do the sharpening in the vise. For finished flies, use the hone during slack times, such as when you're watching TV. If the sharpening must be done on the water, do it before knotting the fly onto the line; if you break the point while sharpening, time won't be lost. Simply set that fly aside and grab another one. —**C.M.**

214. Save Fish and Flies

Much has been made over the advantage of using barbless hooks to minimize wear and tear on fish. A bonus is that barbless hooks also save wear and tear on flies. When a barb is lodged in a fish's jaw, the resulting twisting and jerking, particularly with a hemostat, can be devastating to a delicate fly, often destroying it after only a couple of hookups. The ease of removal of a barbless hook, and the saving on flies, more than compensates for an occasional lost fish. —**C.M.**

215. A Real Hang-up

Returning home late from a long trip, we've all forgotten to remove our waders from their carry bag, leaving them to suffer the ravages of rot, mildew, and funky smells. Keeping waders folded also can cause creasing. Make a point to put them on a hanger as soon as possible. The same applies to wading boots. Get them out into the open to dry. The result will be an extra season of wear, not to mention a more aromatic storage space. —**C.M.**

216. Felt on the Wane

Alarm over the transmission of whirling disease (WD), Didymo, and other invasive organisms deadly to fish populations has caused a backlash against the use of felt on boot soles. Tests have identified felt, for years the standard for no-slip wading, as a prime vehicle in transporting organisms. This prompted New Zealand to ban felt outright; stateside agencies have also voiced concern. Trout Unlimited has called for a moratorium.

Leading bootmaker Simms, in partnership with Italian manufacturer Vibram, has responded with a special synthetic tread design called "RiverTread," which provides good gripping qualities while washing clean. Other manufacturers are following suit.

If you are most comfortable in felt, take the time to clean your boots with a solution of water and Formula 409 before traveling from one river to another (and/or dedicate one set of felt boots to your local river, and travel with rubber soles). That said, the writing is on the wall, and the sooner you learn to wade comfortably on rubber soles, the more options you'll have in the future. —**C.M.**

217. **Doing Our Part**

To a certain extent, we've become victims of our own angling success and mobility. All this running around to distant places has contributed to the spread of organisms such as WD,

Didymo, and various forms of mussels and snails whose microscopic larvae are virtually impossible to detect.

Each of us has a part in protecting our waters, and our angling opportunities. Learn more about these threats in the places you fish and follow environmentally friendly protocols. —C.M.

218. Lose the Sheep

Many fly vests or pouches have fly keepers that were originally made from wool, and are now more often made of foam. While ostensibly providing a handy platform for drying flies or keeping oft-used patterns handy, they help you lose and abuse flies instead. In our preoccupation with the unfolding events of the day, the flies are left hanging to be crushed out of shape or, more likely, dislodged and lost by an excited swipe of a forearm. It's entirely likely more flies have been lost off these keepers than on all the willow limbs of the world.

Unless you're certain you're going to use a fly again in short minutes, it's better to put it back in the box. Better yet, remove the sheepskin or its derivative from the vest so you can avoid the temptation of using it. —C.M.

219. Getting into the Loop

Using loops to connect leaders to fly line or to join pieces of large-diameter monofilament can be a real time-saver, particularly during conditions when normal knot-tying is difficult, such as in extremely low light. Having a pre-tied loop system ready to install can avoid lost time and frustration, particularly for older anglers fighting the inevitable eyesight battle. —C.M.

220. **Getting a Leg Up**

Many anglers complain of lower back pain after a long day casting from a drift boat or peering out across the flats. The reason can often be traced to poor posture caused by over-bending the lower back, accentuating the natural curvature, and pinching the discs between the vertebrae. To avoid this, place an object such as a small block of wood beneath one foot. This will cause the back to straighten, and it will reduce the strain.

The same principle is behind foot railings installed on bars; they're there to keep patrons comfortable while standing for long periods of time, thus drinking more. Translated to fishing, the payoff is pain-free hours of activity. —**C.M.**

221. **A Weighty Alternative**

The standard technique of placing a split shot on the leader above a single or double nymph rig has the disadvantage of causing a hinge in the line and, often, the loss of the entire rig when the weight catches on bottom. Try placing the weight at the bottom of the leader instead.

To do this, tie an overhand knot at the bottom of the line, then pinch on the weight just above it. Tie the flies off on short dropper tippets placed at the desired distance off bottom. A hint: Use a piece of lighter tipper material below the bottom fly, so only this line breaks if it snags, thus losing just the weight, not the flies. Another advantage is that these rigs can be tied ahead of time, ready to be attached with a single blood knot. —**C.M.**

222. Made in the Shade

While paying attention to color and camouflage is a benefit under any light condition, it works even better if an angler can find a casting position in the shade. All other things being equal, choose to fish the shady side of the stream to avoid spooking trout. Also consider that trout don't like looking up into the sun, so most of their rises to dry flies are likely to in shady spots. Trout are also less likely to spot the fraud in the fly with the diminished light. —**C.M.**

223. Backs to the Water

Ponds or lakes tightly surrounded by trees pose a challenging casting problem. Even the closest quarters offer a few openings for a backcast, however. The trick is to find them, not easy with a standard approach that doesn't allow for vision in the backs of our heads. When confronted with such a situation, turn around, face the shore, and then aim your false casts into the gaps. When it's time to deliver, simply turn back toward the water and let fly. This proves the old Lefty Kreh adage that a backcast is simply a forward cast going the other way. A bit of practice will deliver safe casts with little or no loss of distance. —**C.M.**

224. **Dance a Jig**

All fish, but particularly the larger, wiser ones, grow wary of nymphs and streamers stripped straight through the water, which is how most anglers do it. Vary the retrieve so the fly moves up and down in an erratic motion, the sort of action spin fishermen strive for when using jig-style lures.

To make this fish-catching motion easier to achieve, some innovative fly designers tie still-water streamers on bullet-head hooks or actual jig heads. —**C.M.**

225. **Shadow Casting**

The deadly combination of bright sunshine and a calm surface creates line shadows that spook fish. One way to avoid this is to position your cast so the line's shadow doesn't pass over the fish during delivery. When this isn't possible, or when the sun is directly overhead, consider using a roll cast instead. Measure the distance so that only the monofilament leader passes over the fish. —**C.M.**

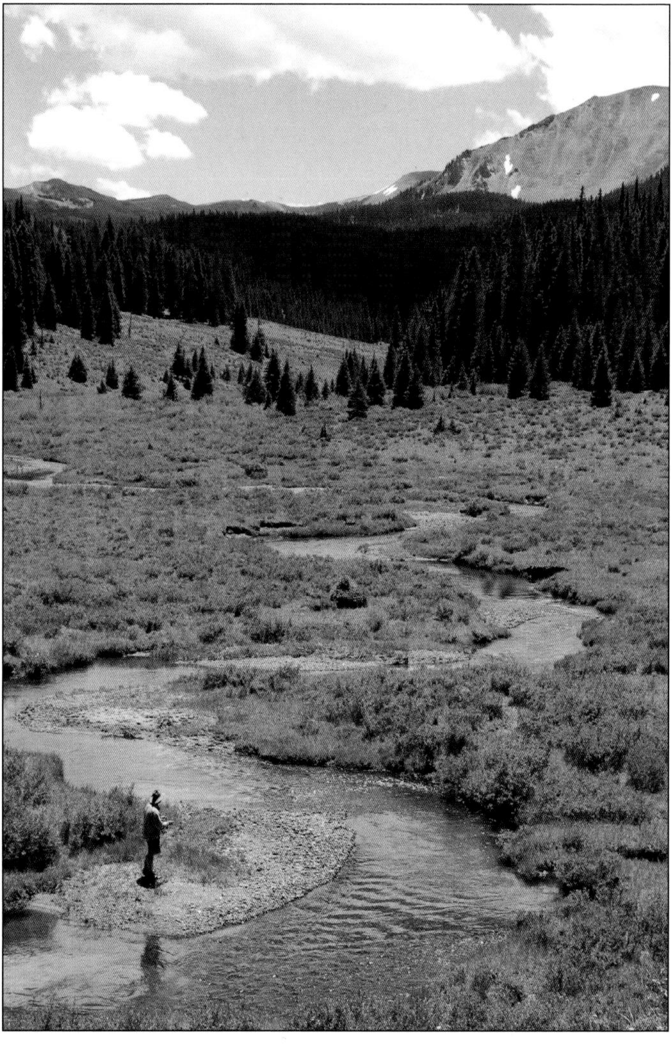

226. Reel Handle Down

Large fish running at full speed can rip loose line rapidly from the deck, often tossing a coil over the reel handle. The result is a spectacular, yet crushing, break off. The solution is simple. Immediately upon hookup, turn the reel so the handle is facing down while feeding line out through the guides with your free hand. —**C.M.**

227. Bow to the King

Once the line has played out and a solid connection is made to that great fish, there's still one major peril remaining, a lesson saltwater anglers learn early on when playing leaping fish such as tarpon. It applies to large trout, steelhead, and salmon as well. When in the air, a fish can contort its body radically, snapping the leader if the line is tight.

To counter this, it's essential to give slack on these leaps, and the best way to achieve that quickly is to dip the rod tip. One way to remember this is to bend briskly at the waist, as in a bow to royalty—which, of course, fits a magnificent fish well enough. —**C.M.**

228. The Knots You Need

You can effectively fly fish for trout your entire life, on any river, in any condition, knowing only three knots: the Nail Knot, which you use to connect your leader to a fly line; the Double Surgeon's Knot, which you use to connect strands of tippet together and lengthen your rig; and the Improved Clinch

Knot, which you use to tie your fly to the tippet. Here's how to tie them:

Two other knots worth knowing are the Blood Knot, which you can use to connect leader and tippet sections (I prefer a Blood Knot over the Surgeon's Knot when I'm using heavier tippets); and the Perfection Loop, used to create a loop-to-loop means of attaching leaders to fly lines. Here's how to tie them:

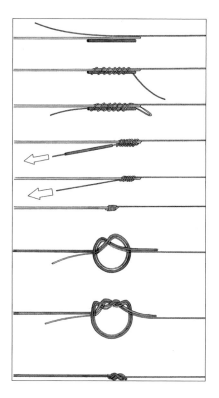

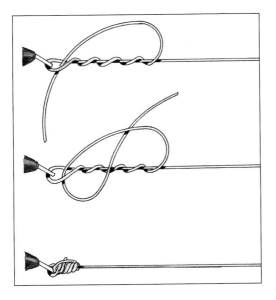

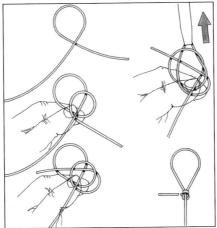

Everything else is pretty much gravy. Saltwater fishing demands a deeper understanding of more complex knots and attachments. Trout fishing does not. Better to learn a few knots well, so you can tie them quickly. Speed trumps strength in most trout situations. —**K.D.**

229. Stepping Down on Tippet

When paring down on tippet sizes, it's best to make the transition as subtle as possible. Don't attach a strand of 5X tippet directly to a piece of beefy 2X; that's a knot waiting to break, due to the awkward, incompatible mesh of materials. Better to tie three knots to taper down: 2X to 3X, 3X to 4X, then 4X to 5X. The biggest tippet jump you should ever take is two sizes, say 3X to 5X, and only do that in a pinch. It's worth the extra time it takes to taper down properly. —**K.D.**

230. 7X Is for Sissies

Very rarely will you ever encounter a situation where the fish are genuinely tippet-shy—where using 7X will catch fish, while using 5X will not with the same fly. If you are getting refused, check the fly pattern first, and more often than not, you should size the fly down. After that, think about your drift and presentation. Odds are you're dragging the fly, regardless of the tippet size. Perhaps you have too much flotant on your fly. Maybe there are weeds on the fly. Tippet is the last thing I'll change when I find extra finicky fish. A good drag-free drift with 4X tippet is far more effective than a sloppy presentation with 7X. Don't use tippet size as a crutch. Make better presentations with heavier tippets, and you will keep more fish buttoned on after they eat your fly. —**K.D.**

231. **Spit on Your Knots**

My mother told me never to spit in public, but I consider spitting on a knot (at least popping the tippet into my mouth) before I cinch it down an exception to the rule. Always wet your knots; it makes the connection tighter and stronger. —**K.D.**

232. **Hang Your Weight above a Knot**

After putting together a nymph rig and fishing it a few times, many anglers find that the weight has slid down on top of their fly. Rather than pinch the weight on tighter, take the extra step of strategically placing a surgeon's knot on your tippet about a foot above your first fly. Pinch the weight onto the tippet above that knot, and you're guaranteed that it won't slide down onto your fly anymore. —**K.D.**

233. **Cast Across a Snag**

You're going to snag your flies in one of two places: in front of you, or behind you. If you don't occasionally snag flies on obstacles in front (trees, rocks, and so on), you aren't trying hard enough. If you often snag your flies behind you, you aren't thinking hard enough.

To free flies from snags in front of you, strip line off the reel and punch a cast over the snag so that several feet of line lands on the other side. Then give the line a sharp pop backward. If it's not wrapped up or sunk too deeply in the snag, your fly will pull loose as the reverse momentum backs the hook out in the same direction it stuck. —**K.D.**

234. **Get the Lead Out**

Lead is poison. It's poisonous for people, it's poisonous for birds, and it's poisonous for animals that live in or around lakes, ponds, and rivers. Think about that the next time you have a split shot washing around in your mouth as you finger through the fly box.

Tin, tungsten, and other metals work just as well as, if not better than, lead. —**K.D.**

235. **Tap the Rod**

Here's a slick trick that will impress your fishing friends and make life easier: When moving from one spot to another, always keep the fly line-to-leader connection pulled through the tip top of your rod. Trying to pull the knot through the end

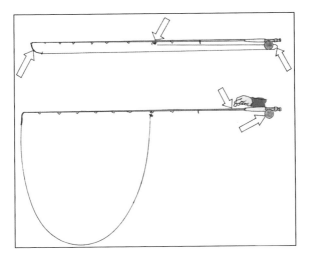

guide in a hurry with bent rod on the stream is a pain, and is also a good way to break the tip.

With the knot through the tip top, hang your bottom fly on a guide halfway up the rod, drape the leader around the reel seat, and reel in the slack so the fly line connection remains outside the guides.

When you are ready to fish, undrape the leader from behind your reel, let the line hang free, then give a gentle tap or two on the top of the rod, just above the cork handle. The slight vibration will pop the fly off the guide, and your line will fall into the water. No reaching up the rod and picking the flies off (or sticking your fingers). Let it hang, give it a tap, and you're good to go. —**K.D.**

236. How to Net a Fish

Colorado guide Tom Whitley literally nets fish for a living. As we all know, this is where many hooked trout get away.

Here are the keys, according to Whitley. First, note the fish's body position. Tilted at a 45-degree angle (head pointed toward the bottom) and finning away wildly, the fish isn't ready for the net. To make that fish ready, drop the rod parallel to the water surface, maintain a solid bend in the rod, and steer the fish toward you.

At the critical moment when your fish is within reach, abruptly lift the rod tip skyward, changing the angle of the fish so that its head points upward. When this happens, or when the fish's head breaks the surface, maintain that tension and control. The trout has lost his leverage, and that's when you can scoop him with the net. —**K.D.**

237. Fish Handling 101

There are two things to keep in mind when you are handling and releasing trout. First, wet your hands so you don't damage the slime layer on the trout's skin, which actually serves as a defense against disease and other maladies.

Second, take the time to bend down and handle the fish close to the water surface. If you drop a wiggling fish a few inches into water, no harm, no foul. Pull a fish to standing eye level, then accidentally drop it onto the rocks, and you might just have well have dropped it into a creel. —**K.D.**

238. Make the Camera Work for You

Most advice about fishing photography involves how to capture spectacular scenery or make your fish look bigger than it really is. When fishing mountain reservoirs, consider another use for the camera, one that might produce a trout that doesn't need photographic exaggeration. These impoundments were constructed for water supply, which means they'll be drained down sometimes during the year, revealing boulders, drop-offs, and other structure. That's when you should take out your camera and shoot all of the fish-holding irregularities. When the reservoir refills, you'll have pictures of the most likely places to cast. —**C.M.**

239. Hold Your Breath for Photos

We all like to take the occasional photographs of our fishing adventures. Just remember this simple tip when doing so. When you take a fish out of water, start holding your breath.

When you feel a bit uncomfortable, odds are the fish does too, and it's time to put it back in the water to get oxygen flowing through its gills. —**K.D.**

240. God Save the Queen

It happens to all of us. You see a trout rise to your dry fly, and in the excitement of the moment, you go to set the hook, but only succeed in ripping the fly off the surface before the trout grabs it in earnest. Stung or not, that trout is now smarter and usually won't fall for your act anymore.

In situations like this, you have to force yourself to be patient. You must let the trout not only rise to the fly, but chomp down on it before you set the hook. This is especially true when you are fishing terrestrials like hoppers, ants, and beetles.

In New Zealand, where the trout are big and dry-fly takes are hard-earned, they have a system to make every rise count: When that fish bubbles up and eats the fly, they say (aloud or otherwise), "God Save the Queen," and then set the hook.

Do the same thing. If you aren't a loyal subject of the Commonwealth, substitute the old cadence for rushing the quarterback in a flag football game—one-Mississippi, two-Mississippi—and then give the trout the business. Hum the first notes of Beethoven's Fifth Symphony . . . whatever it takes. But find a system, audible in your mind, to build pause between rise and hook-set, and you will land more, and educate fewer, trout. —**K.D.**

241. Trout Hook-Set: Answer the Telephone

How hard should you set the hook when a trout eats your fly? If you don't set it hard enough, the fish gets away; set it too hard, and you break off.

The advice I give to novice anglers is to set the hook with essentially the same speed, force, and range of motion as answering the telephone. You lift the receiver off the desk, and bring the phone directly to your ear. Pick it up the rod handle with purpose, and pull it even to your ear: No more, no less. Do it all in one steady, deliberate, swift (but not violent) stroke.

Answer the phone, and say hello to more hooked trout. —K.D.

242. Web Sites

The modern angler has an incredible advantage at his or her fingertips: the Internet. It used to be that the only way to know what shape the river was in and what the trout were eating was

to go to the water and check it out in person. Now, if you want to know if the Hendricksons are hatching on the upper Delaware, it takes five minutes to get the scoop. Simply go to the Web sites of fly shops in the area, and you'll know what's going on.

That said, don't let the patter generated by some guy blogging in his basement dictate all your choices. Consider your sources carefully. Start with the info from the local fly shop (and the smart ones have Web sites that get updated regularly). —**K.D.**

243. Cut and Re-tie Knotted Tippet

How many times have you noticed a tiny wind knot on your tippet or leader, and figured it's not a big deal? What usually happens is that you make a few more casts, inevitably hook a big fish, and break clean off.

Even the smallest knot in your tippet can severely diminish the strength of your connection. You almost always pay for laziness. If you notice a knot, cut the tippet and re-rig. It took me 10 years of paying for my stubbornness to figure out it's always best to have an optimal rig working. After all, you never know how big, how tough, and how smart the next fish you hook will be. —**K.D.**

244. Lotions and Bug Spray

Lotions and DEET-laden insect repellents will eat right through many fly lines. If you want to keep the skeeters away, great, just be sure you aren't spraying your line or handling it with gooey fingers. —**K.D.**

245. **On Etiquette**

This book would not serve its mission without at least some guidance on stream etiquette. Not that fly fishing needs a rule book; nevertheless, some basic ethos should be followed in order to make the experience better for everyone.

Don't jump in the same run that someone else is fishing. Same bank, opposite bank, whatever, do not fish the same run unless you are invited to do so.

Assume another angler is working from downstream up. No matter how the person is fishing, you can figure that most good anglers will be moving upstream.

Looking at a river, you can usually see the runs where trout will be. It's good form to leave any angler you encounter at least two or three runs above where you find him fishing, before you think about dropping in the river. (In a crowded stream—say, New York's Beaverkill on a Saturday in May—this may be impractical. At the least, give other anglers their space.)

If you park at a public access area and don't want to be crowded, consider leaving notice of your intentions. Put a sign on your windshield—"I'm fishing upstream-down," or "I'm fishing 400 yards downstream, back up"—to give anglers arriving after you a fair warning of your intentions.

Don't fish posted, private water. If you do so, you're a poacher.

And don't make your comments and conversation a part of another angler's experience unless he or she wants it to be.

Play by these few simple rules, and everyone has a good time. —**K.D.**

246. What Did I Do Wrong?

I'm on a guide trip. My client has just hooked into a monster brown trout. He fights a pitched battle for several minutes, then the fish comes loose. Game over. Ninety-nine percent of the time, the crestfallen angler looks back at me and asks the same thing: "What did I do wrong?"

If the tippet is broken, the answer is obvious: Too much pressure. But if the fish simply spit the fly, and throughout the fight I noted that the angler had good even pressure on the fish, 99 percent of the time my answer is, "Nothing."

Those things happen. It's a part of fishing. Nobody should expect to land them all. —**K.D.**

247. Take the Reins

When you hook a fish, the thing most people (rightly) think about is keeping that rod tip high. Good. But if you're in or near heavy current, you also want to steer that fish toward the

bank. If you let a strong trout play *you* out in heavy current, even with a high rod tip, the trout is at an advantage unless you are able to exert some will and influence its direction.

Watch a good angler work a hooked trout, and you'll notice it doesn't take all that long for him to land it. That's good for both the angler, who will ultimately land more fish, and the trout, which will be subjected to a lower level of exhaustion.

The key is to dip the rod toward the bank and force the fish toward slack water. It's like steering a horse with reins. Tip the rod right, turn the fish right; tip the rod left, turn him left. When the fish is ready for the net, that's when you go back high with the rod tip. Start and end the fight with a high tip. In between, you dictate the action by steering side to side. —**K.D.**

248. **Be Ambidextrous**

The more you develop your casting and reeling abilities with your "off" hand, the better fly fisherman you'll become. Here's a simple way to start developing a cast with your non-dominant hand, shared by guide and writer Kim Leighton on the Yellowstone River years ago:

Cast as you normally would, using your dominant hand, but as you do this, gently cup the reel with your off hand. This will build a sense of timing and tempo that you can eventually transfer from one hand to the other. If you're only able to develop a casting ability with your off hand that is 25 percent of your good one, you'll still better off when you find yourself in a tough spot where the river, cover, and currents make an opposite-arm delivery your only viable option. —**K.D.**

249. The Tail Gunner

Fishing from a drift boat is one of the most enjoyable experiences in fly fishing. You see the sights, you cover water, and you can catch many fish. But there's nothing more frustrating for an oarsman than having two people regularly tangling their lines (and this inevitably happens right when you approach the honey hole, as instinct and anticipation hijack your common sense).

Here's a simple rule that solves that problem: If lines get tangled, it's the person in the back of the boat who's at fault. Period. No arguments or excuses allowed.

The "tail gunner" has the ability to watch everything unfolding in front of him. It's his responsibility to watch the angler in the bow, and time his casts accordingly. In time, you'll grow to enjoy the tail gunner's seat. You're the quarterback of the three-person team. You're batting cleanup. And every now and again you'll make that hero hookup where the front person missed. —**K.D.**

250. The Most Important Tip

None of this book will have mattered if you don't take at least some of this information and pass it on to another angler— a son, daughter, grandchild, friend, or someone you happen to bump into on the river who asks for a little advice.

We said at the start of this book that you might not agree with everything we have covered. By its very nature, fly fishing is an evolving, flowing gray mass, like a river. There are no absolute certainties, only suggestions. Hopefully, some of our tips will help you get more out of the sport.

But both of us can tell you from experience that to really get something out of fly fishing, you need to share it. Pass it on. Every angler should endeavor to replace himself.

One of the criticisms outdoor writers face is that our job is all about spilling the beans. We kiss and tell for a living. And we're fine with that, for the reward is watching the fly-fishing passion take root in other people.

A fishing guide isn't doing his job unless he leaves a client with at least one lesson that makes him a better angler, regardless of how many fish are taken on a given day. To a large degree, the same can be said of any fly fisherman. It's all about passing it on. If we don't, who will preserve our trout waters in the future?

Ultimately, what you have here are insights from two fly fishing and outdoor writing careers. It's our lifeblood, caught and released to you. It's our hope that you will take these tips, use them, catch fish, enjoy fly fishing, add some insights of your own, and release all of that experience to others. —**K.D. & C.M.**